IMAGINE A WOMAN
AND OTHER TALES

Imagine a Woman and Other Tales

Richard Selzer

Michigan State University Press
East Lansing

Grateful acknowledgment is made to the Houghton Library, The New York Public Library, the Henry W. and Albert A. Berg Collection and the Astor, Lenox, and Tilden Foundations for permission to adapt the fragment "The Light-House" by Edgar Allan Poe. Reprinted by permission of the Houghton Library, The New York Public Library, the Henry W. and Albert A. Berg Collection and the Astor, Lenox, and Tilden Foundations.

The story "Whither Thou Goest" was originally published as "Follow Your Heart" in the September 1990 issue of *Redbook*.

First Michigan State University Press printing, 1996.

All Michigan State University Press books are produced on paper which meets the requirements of American National Standard of Information Sciences—Permanence of paper for printed materials ANSI Z39.48-1984.

Michigan State University Press
East Lansing, Michigan 48823-5202

ISBN 0-87013-458-2

02 01 00 99 98 97 96 1 2 3 4 5 6 7 8 9

Library of Congress Cataloging-in-Publication Data

Selzer, Richard.
       Imagine a woman and other tales / by Richard Selzer.
              p.   cm.
       I. Title
PS3569.E585147 1990
813'.54—dc20   90-53124

For my grandchildren,
Becky Lehman and Henry Ash Selzer

CONTENTS

WHITHER THOU GOEST

"Brain-dead," said the doctor. "There is no chance that he will wake up. Ever. Look here." And he unrolled a scroll of paper onto her lap.

"This is the electroencephalograph. It's nothing but a flat line. No blips." Hannah bowed her head over the chart. The doctor cleared his throat, took one of her hands in both of his, and leaned toward her as though about to tell a secret. Hannah submitted to what under any other circumstances she might have considered presumption, submitted because she thought she ought to. It was expected of her. The formality of the occasion and all.

"Hannah, it is three weeks since your husband was shot in the head. The only thing keeping him alive is the respirator."

Hannah waited for the walls of the solarium to burst.

"I'm asking you to let us put an end to it, unplug the machinery, let him go. There is just no sense in prolonging a misfortune." Hannah felt that she should say something, not just sit there, but for the life of her she couldn't think what. The doctor was speaking again.

"But before we do that, we would like your permission to harvest Sam's organs for transplantation."

"Harvest?" said Hannah. "Like the gathering in of wheat?"

"Yes," said the doctor. "That is what we call it when we take the organs. It is for a good cause. That way your husband will live on. He will not really have died . . ."

"Dead is dead," said Hannah.

"I know, I know," said the doctor. And he looked down at his feet for relief. Hannah noticed that he was wearing oxblood wing-tip shoes of a large size. They were the shoes of power.

A week later she received a letter from the doctor.

Dear Mrs. Owen,

You will be pleased and comforted to know that because of your generosity and thanks to the miracle of modern science, seven people right here in the state of Texas are living and well with all their faculties restored to them. Your husband's liver has gone to a lady in Abilene; the right kidney is functioning in Dallas; the left kidney was placed in a teenaged girl in Galveston; the heart was given to a man just your husband's age in a little town near Arkansas; the lungs are in Fort Worth; and the corneas were used on two people right here in Houston. . . .

Hannah folded the letter and put it back in its envelope and then into the bottom drawer of the desk without reading to the end. There was no need. She already knew what had become of the rest of Sam. She had buried it in the family plot of the Evangelical Baptist Church cemetery.

▼   ▼   ▼

That was three years ago. And still, she had only to close her eyes to have the whole of the horror spring vividly before her, as though it had been painted on the inside of her eyelids. For Sam's thirty-third birthday they had spent the weekend at the beach. Now they were in the pickup truck on the way back to Houston. Hannah had fallen asleep. It was the sudden stop that woke her up.

"We couldn't be there already," she murmured.

"No," said Sam. "I'm just going to change that lady's tire." Hannah sat up and saw the green Buick pulled off to the side of the road. The right rear tire was flat. An elderly woman sitting behind the wheel looked up and smiled when she saw Sam walking toward her with a car jack in one hand and the tire iron in the other. Hannah got out of the truck and went over to talk. "Bless you," the woman said. Sam hadn't given that jack more than half a dozen pumps when a man—he looked Mexican—appeared out of nowhere with a gun in his hand.

"Sam?" Hannah had said in that low, questioning voice that always made him turn to see if she was upset. For a long moment Sam stayed where he was, crouched over the jack. When at last he stood, he had the tire iron in his hand.

"What do you want, mister?" he said. The Mexican made a gesture as if to turn a key and nodded at the pickup.

"The keys are in the truck," said Sam. The Mexican made no move. Perhaps he did not understand? Sam raised his arm to point. The Mexican fired. It took a long time for the echo of that shot to peter out. When it had, the truck and the Mexican were gone, and Sam lay on his back wearing a halo of black blood. He was still holding the tire iron. Something pink squeezed slowly out of the middle of his forehead.

"Dead is dead," she had told that doctor. But now, three years later, she wasn't so sure. For Hannah had begun to have doubts. Incidents occurred, like the time months ago when she had gone to the butcher's. Just ahead of her at the counter a woman had ordered a chicken. "I want it in parts," she heard the woman say. Hannah had watched as the butcher scooped out the entrails, cleaved the carcass through the middle of the breast, and hacked off its thighs, legs, and wings. The heart, gizzard, neck, and liver he put in a small plastic bag.

"You can keep the feet," said the woman. And then it was Hannah's turn.

"What'll it be?" said the butcher. And wiped the clots from his fingers onto his apron.

"What do you call that?" she asked, trying not to look at his bloody hands. As though they were his privates.

"What do you call what?"

"What you just did, cutting up the chicken. What is the name for it?" The butcher stared at her blankly.

"It's called 'cleaning a chicken.' Why?"

"Cleaning?"

"Look, miss," said the butcher, "I'm real busy. What'll it be?" But Hannah had already turned to leave.

It was after that that she stopped going to the cemetery to visit the grave. It wasn't Sam in that cemetery, not by a long shot. It was only parts of Sam, the parts that nobody needed. The rest of him was scattered all over Texas. And, unless she had been misinformed, very much alive. And where did that leave her? God knows it was hard enough to be a widow at the age of thirty-three, and her sympathies were all with those women whose husbands had truly, once and for all, died. But widowhood, bleak as it might be, seemed preferable by a whole lot to the not-here, not-there condition into which she had been thrust by "the miracle of modern science." At least if your husband were all dead you could one day get over it and go on with your life. But this! This state of bafflement. Maybe, she thought, maybe it was a matter of percentage—if more than 50 percent of your husband was dead, you were a widow. Whom could she ask?

Along with doubt came resentment. Oh, not just at the doctors. They simply do what they want to anyway, without really thinking. Doctors, she decided, don't think. They just *do*, and cover it all up with language. *Harvest. Transplantation.* The soft words of husbandry and the soil. Even they cannot bear to speak the real names of their deeds—dismemberment, evisceration. What was worse, she had begun to resent Samuel. Here she was, living in this sort of limbo, while he, Sam, was participating in not one but seven lives, none of which had anything to do with her. It wasn't fair. Even if he hadn't chosen it, it wasn't fair.

▼　　　▼　　　▼

Hannah's cousin Ivy Lou was also her best friend. Lately she had taken to bringing her lunch over to eat at Hannah's house. One day when she got there, Hannah was standing at the kitchen window, looking out into the backyard. Over the radio came the pitched monotone of a preacher. The subject was the resurrection of the flesh.

"And it says right here in First Corinthians, chapter fifteen: 'For the trumpet shall sound, and the dead shall be raised incorruptible.'

"And here it is again in Romans, chapter eight, verse eleven: 'If the Spirit of him who raised Jesus from the dead dwells in you, he who raised Christ Jesus from the dead will give life to your mortal bodies . . .'"

"Turn that damn fool off," said Hannah.

"For goodness sake!" said Ivy Lou. "What's got into you?" Four years ago Ivy Lou had been born again.

"It's a big lie," said Hannah. "It's the way the preachers swindle you."

"I'm sure I don't know what you are talking about," said Ivy Lou.

"There is no such thing as the resurrection of the flesh," said Hannah. "Just tell me at what stage of life we are supposed to be on the day of resurrection, so-called? Do we look as we did when we were babies? At age forty? Or as we are when we die, old and wasted? And tell me this: What about Samuel Owen on your resurrection day? Here he is scattered all over Texas, breathing in Fort Worth, urinating in Dallas *and* Galveston, digesting or whatever it is the liver does in Abilene. They going to put him back together again when the day comes, or is it to the recipients belong the spoils? Tell me that."

"Well," said Ivy Lou. "I don't have the least idea about any of that, but I do know that you are committing the sin of blasphemy. Hannah, I'm real worried about you. Don't you believe in God anymore?" Hannah looked out the window and was silent for a long moment.

"About God," she said at last, "I have only the merest inkling. That's all anyone can have."

▼   ▼   ▼

Hannah could not have said exactly when the idea first occurred to her. Later, she thought it might have been on the day of the tornado. From the kitchen window her eye had been caught by a frenzy of leaves in the live oak. All that August morning it had been sultry and still, until all at once it turned dark as twilight. Then lightning came to tear open the clouds. And the air, as if desperate to announce great tidings, broke its silence and turned to wind. But such a wind! At the height of the storm Hannah opened the back door and stood to receive the force of the rain on her face, her hair. It stung like pebbles. The violence lasted but a few minutes, after which it settled into a steady drizzle. Then, as abruptly as it had come, the storm passed and the sun came out, leaving Hannah with the feeling that something more than the humidity had been relieved. Something, a pressure that had been building inside her, had boiled its way to the surface, then broke.

That very night she awoke suddenly and sat bolt upright in bed, and she clapped her hand over her mouth as if to hold back what threatened to burst forth from it. A scream? Laughter? She didn't know what. But what she did know, beyond any doubt, as though it had been a revelation, was what it was she must do.

She had been dreaming, and in her dream, she saw two men lying on narrow tables next to each other. One of them was Samuel; the other she could not see clearly. His features were blurred, out of focus. Both of the men were stripped to the waist, and their chests were open in the middle, the halves of their rib cages raised like cellar doors. A surgeon was there, dressed in a blue scrub suit, mask, and cap. As she watched, the surgeon reached his hands into Samuel's chest and lifted forth his heart, held it up like some luminous prize. At that moment, Hannah could see into the chests of both men, see that they were both empty. Then the surgeon turned away from Samuel and lowered the incandescent, glowing heart into the chest of the other man, who promptly sat up, put on his shirt, and walked away.

What was instantly made clear to her—it was so simple—was that she must go to find that man who was carrying Samuel's heart. If she could find him, and listen once more to the heart, she would be healed. She would be able to go on with her life.

In the morning, the idea seemed quite mad. She wondered whether she was losing her mind. And she began to interrogate herself. Why would she do such a thing? What good would it do? To say nothing of the intrusion on the life of a perfect stranger. What made her think he would agree to let her do it? How could she explain it to him when she could not even explain it to herself? What would she say? Would it be like a pilgrim visiting a shrine? No, it had nothing to do with worship. Although, it might be a bit like going to the Delphic oracle for advice. But that wasn't it either. Did she just want to make sure that Sam's heart had found a good home? For God's sake, it wasn't a dog that she had given away. Nor was she the least bit curious about the man himself, other than to know how to find him. "No," Hannah said aloud, addressing the nameless, faceless man of her dream. "Thou shalt be unto my hand as a banister upon a dark staircase, to lead me up to the bright landing above. Once having climbed, I shall most willingly let thee go." The more she thought about it, the more she felt like a woman whose husband had been declared missing in action in a war. What would she have done if that were the case? Why, she would bend every effort to find him—living or dead—even travel to Vietnam or Laos, wherever, and she wouldn't leave until she knew, one way or the other.

Perhaps it *was* a phantom she was chasing, a phantom that would dissolve when she drew near. But she would have to take that chance. Hannah remembered the time, a year after they were married, when she and Samuel were lying in bed and she had said:

"Let's tell each other a secret. You first." And Sam had told her about when he was twelve years old and his father had died suddenly of a heart attack. For a long time afterward he would think that he saw his father on the streets of the city. It was always from the back, so he couldn't be sure. But the man was wearing the same gray fedora and holding the cigarette the same way. The more Sam looked, the more certain he became that it was his father whom he saw walking downtown, that he had not really died, but had gone away or been taken away from some reason, and now here he was. And Samuel would quicken his pace, then break into a run to catch up, calling out "Daddy! Daddy!" in his excitement. And each time, when the man turned around to see, it wasn't, no it wasn't, and there was that fresh wave of desolation. One day, a policeman came to the door and told his mother that Sam had been following men on the street and that one of them had reported him, said he might be a pickpocket, or worse.

"Is it true?" asked his mother. When he didn't answer, she asked him why. But he couldn't or wouldn't say why because no one would believe him or understand, and they would think he was crazy.

"Well, don't you dare do it ever again," said his mother in front of the policeman. But he couldn't stop, because the next day he thought he saw his father again and he followed him. After a year it stopped happening and Sam felt a mixture of relief and disappointment. Relief, because at last he had laid to rest his father's ghost; disappointment, because the wild possibility no longer existed. Sam had never told anyone about this before, he said. It was the first time he had ever mentioned it. When he had finished, Hannah hugged him and kissed him and cried and cried for the young boy who couldn't let go of his father.

"You're so pretty," Sam had said after a while to make her stop.

But Sam had been a young boy, and she was a grown woman. No matter—even if it turned out that she, too, was chasing a phantom.

Hannah went to the cupboard where three years before she had placed the doctor's letter, the one telling her about the seven transplantations. She read it again, this time to the end, and made a list. The kidneys, liver, and lungs, she decided, were inaccessible—hidden away in the deepest recesses of the bodies of those who had received them. How could she get to them? And the corneas just didn't seem right. She didn't think she could relate to a cornea. That left the heart. A heart can be listened to. A heart can be felt. And besides, there had been her dream. She would seek to follow the heart. But then there was that man, that other, who had lain on the table next to Samuel and whose face she had not been able to see. What if he refused her, mistook her intentions? No, she would explain it to him, write it all in a letter, and then he would agree. He would have to. In the letter she would tell what happened that night on the highway, how Sam had raised his arm to point to the truck, still holding the tire iron, how the Mexican had fired, and what the doctor had said to her in the hospital.

"That way your husband will not really have died," he had said. And that she had said to him, "Dead is dead," but that now she was not so sure. And how, ever since, she had been living in this gray place, unable to grieve or get on with her life because she no longer knew who or even what she was. All this she would tell him in the letter and he would let her come. He must.

▼   ▼   ▼

Once she had decided, it was not difficult to get his name and address, a few of the facts of his illness. Hospital records, she learned, were scandalously accessible to whoever might want to see them, whatever the hospitals swore to the contrary. Anyone who really tried could get to see them—lawyers hunting for malpractice suits, legal assistants, reporters, detectives, graduate students gathering statistics, nurses, insurance companies. It was in this last guise that Hannah called the record librarian of the university hospital and made an appointment. She had followed it up with a letter on official stationery of the Aetna Casualty and Life Insurance Company.

She had had to take Ivy Lou into her confidence; Ivy Lou worked as a secretary for Aetna.

Ivy Lou was appalled. "I don't like it one bit. No good will come of it." And at first she had refused. "I just don't see what you could possibly hope to get out of it." And then, when Hannah didn't answer, "Why? Just tell me why."

"I don't know why," said Hannah. How could she say why, when she really didn't know herself? Perhaps it was something like the way a flower can't help but face the sun, or the way a moth goes to the flame.

"Hannah, you're going to get burned," said Ivy Lou as though she had read her mind. "Besides," she went on, "it's not only sick, it's in the grossest ill taste." Ivy Lou set down her teacup and walked to the door, shaking her head.

But then, there was poor Hannah, and in the end Ivy Lou gave in.

"Just don't tell anyone where you got it," she said when she brought the stationery.

The next week at the hospital, the record librarian welcomed her with a smile and showed her to a cubicle where the chart was waiting for her. POPE, HENRY, she read. AGE: 33. NEXT OF KIN: MRS. INEZ POPE. CHILDREN: NONE. ADDRESS: 8 ORCHARD ROAD, AVERY, TEXAS. DIAGNOSIS: CARDIOMYOPATHY, VIRAL. SURGERY: HEART TRANSPLANT. Reading on, she learned of his "intractable heart failure," that his prognosis had been "hopeless"—he had been given an estimated life expectancy of a few months "at most."

And then she came to the part about the operation, which occupied the bulk of the fat chart, and none of which she read. There was no need.

"That didn't take long," said the librarian as Hannah walked by her desk.

"No," said Hannah. "I'm quick."

▼　　▼　　▼

Avery, Texas. Hannah and Ivy Lou looked for it on a map.

"There it is," said Ivy Lou. "Way up almost into Arkansas."

"How far away is that?"

"Maybe a couple of hundred miles, but, Hannah, I'm telling you—don't. You are making the biggest mistake of your life."

That night, Hannah sat at her kitchen table with a pen and a blank sheet of paper. "Dear Mr. Pope," she wrote, then set down the pen. There was something absurd about that *Mr.*, considering that she had been married for seven years to a significant part of the man. But she would let it stand. The situation called for tact, patience, diplomacy. There would be plenty of time for "Dear Henry," if and when. She picked up the pen and continued.

My name is Hannah Owen. Could the name mean anything to you? Doubtless not, considering the decorum with which these things are done. I am the wife (some say widow) of Samuel Owen, the man whose heart is even now beating in your chest.

Perhaps you will forgive a woman's curiosity? I am writing to ask how you are since the operation. Your early discharge from the intensive-care unit, and even from the hospital itself—three weeks! It might be a record of some kind and would seem to show that you had an uneventful recovery. It would follow that you have continued to improve and that by now, three years later, you have completely regained your health? I surely do hope so. It is my dearest wish that the heart is doing as good a job for you as it did for Sam and for me too. Do let me hear from you, please,

Yours truly,
Hannah Owen

There, she thought. That should do it. Nothing whatever to arouse suspicion or to make anyone wonder. Only the shock of who she was. After that, just an expression of well-meaning concern. When she dropped the letter in the slot at the post office and heard the soft siffle as it went down the chute, she sighed. It had begun.

▼   ▼   ▼

It was too weeks before she saw the envelope in her mailbox written in neat handwriting in black ink. It was postmarked Avery, Texas. How it shook in her hand.

Dear Mrs. Owen,
It was very kind of you to write asking after my husband's health. He is not much of a letter writer and has asked me to tell you that he is stronger and healthier than he has been in years. He says he is the luckiest man on earth. By the way, however did you get hold of our name and address? I had thought such information might be protected, under the circumstances, but—I guess not. Thank you for your interest.

Sincerely,
(Mrs.) Inez Pope

Dear Mr. Pope,
I don't know any other way to say it than to just take a deep breath and come right out with it. What I am going to ask will seem at first quite insane. But I assure you I am no maniac. I want to come and listen to your heart for the space of one hour at a time when it is convenient for you. While I know that at first this request will seem strange to you, I pray that you will say yes. You have no idea how important it is to me.

Yours truly,
Hannah Owen

Dear Mrs. Owen,

My husband and I have tried to understand your position. But we feel that it would not be at all wise for you to come here. Not that we aren't grateful and all of that, but you have to admit it is a little on the bizarre side. So this is good-bye.

Sincerely,
(Mrs.) Henry Pope

P.S. We have consulted with our doctor, who says it is a terrible idea and perhaps you should get some professional attention to get over it. No offense meant.

Dear Mr. Pope,

Your wife does not wish to let me come. I can understand her hesitation. The awkwardness and all. And perhaps it is only human nature, a touch of suspicion. Perhaps I have ulterior motives? I assure you, Mr. Pope, that I do not. As for my interest in you personally, it is limited to you as the carrier of something I used to possess and which I for one reason or another would like to see again. Or rather, hear again. For that is all I want to do— to listen to your heart for the space of one hour. The way a person would like to go back to visit the house where he had grown up. You are in a sense that house. Your doctor doesn't think it is a good idea? Mr. Pope, the doctors don't think. They are unaccustomed to it. Doctors just do whatever they want to, without thinking. If they had thought, perhaps they might have foreseen the predicament into which the "miracle of modern science" has placed me. No, speak to me not of doctors. They haven't the least idea about the human heart except to move it from place to place.

Yours truly,
Hannah Owen

Dear Mrs. Owen,
I am very sorry. But the answer is still no. And that is final. Ever since I got your first letter, I've been feeling awful. Like ungrateful or something. But I know in my heart it wouldn't be a good thing for you either.

Sincerely yours,
Henry Pope

Dear Mr. Pope,
The circumstances of my husband's death were violent and shocking. In case you do not know, he was shot in the head by a bandit on the highway where he had stopped to help an old lady with a flat tire. I was there. After three weeks on the respirator, they came and told me it was no use, and could they disconnect the respirator? But just before they did that, could they take parts of his body (*harvest* is the word) to transplant to other people? I said yes, and so they took his liver, lungs, heart, corneas, and kidneys. There are seven of you out there. You, Mr. Pope, got the heart, or more exactly, *my* heart, as under the law, I had become the owner of my husband's entire body at the time that he became "brain-dead." Don't worry—I don't want it back. But I do ask you to let me come to Avery for one hour to listen to your heart. It is such a small thing, really, to ask in return for the donation of a human heart. Just to listen. For one hour. That is all, really all. The reasons are private, and anyway, even if I wanted to tell you why, I don't know if I could put it into words. If you see fit to let me come, I will never bother you again, and you will have repaid me in full. Do please let me know when I can come.

Yours truly,
Hannah Owen

P.S. Of course your wife can be in the room all the time. Although, frankly, I would prefer otherwise. Mrs. Pope, what I want to do is no more than what dozens of nurses have done—listen to your husband's heart. Only the reason is different. Couldn't you look at it as just another medical checkup?

Dear Mrs. Owen,
You said there were seven of us recipients. Why me? Or do you plan a statewide reunion with all your husband's organs? And the answer is NO! Please do not keep writing, as it is annoying to say the least, and it is making my wife nervous.

Sincerely,
Henry Pope

Dear Mr. Pope,
You ask "Why me?" And you are right to ask. It is because you have the heart. The others—the liver, lungs, kidneys—are hidden away. I can't get to them. As for the corneas, well, I just can't relate to corneas somehow. But the heart! A heart can be felt. It can be listened to. You can hear a heart. A heart is reachable. That's why *you.*

Yours truly,
Helen Owen

When there had been no reply for two weeks, Hannah wrote again.

Dear Mr. Pope,
Please.

Yours truly,
Hannah Owen

Dear Mrs. Owen,
No, goddammit, and if you don't stop this business and get the hell out of my life, I'm going to notify the police.

Sincerely yours,
Henry Pope

Dear Mr. Pope,
And so your answer is still No. Oh, can you imagine how sad I am? Now I am the one who is disheartened. Never mind. I will try to accept it, as I have no alternative. You said I can't come and so I won't. I shall not be bothering you and your wife again. You can relax. I can't resist saying one more time, although it doesn't matter anymore, that I was the owner of the heart. It was mine to give. I think I did mention to you that the body of the deceased is the property of the next of kin. It wasn't Samuel who was the donor at all. It was me. But that is all water over the dam. Now may I ask you for a much smaller favor? I would like to have a photograph of you for my scrapbook. Nothing, for goodness sake, posed or formal. Just a casual snapshot would be fine. Chalk it up to foolish sentiment. Thank you and good-bye.

Yours truly,
Hannah Owen

For three weeks Hannah prowled the house, smoking the cigarettes of disappointment, settling into her despair. Ivy Lou was frankly worried, but she knew better than to suggest a psychiatrist, or a minister, for that matter.

"Hannah," she said, "You have got to pull yourself together and get over it. It was a lousy idea in the first place. What's going to be the end of it?"

"I really don't know," said Hannah and waited for Ivy Lou to go away.

And then there it was, lying at the bottom of her mailbox like a dish of cream waiting to be lapped up. No need to look at the postmark—she could tell that handwriting anywhere. Stifling her excitement, she waited till she was back in her kitchen, sitting at the table, before she opened it. The sole content was a snapshot. No letter.

Hannah studied the photograph. It was three by four inches, black and white. The next size up from passport. It showed, at some distance, a thin, dark-haired man slouched against the trunk of a tree, his right knee flexed at right angles, with the sole of his foot braced against the tree. A live oak, she guessed, judging by the girth. His hands bulged the pockets of a zip-up jacket. He wore a baseball cap and was looking off to the left, the head turned almost in profile. The face, what she could see of it, was unremarkable, the eyes, shaded by the peak of the cap, giving away nothing. Only the dark seam of a mouth expressed suffering. Even with the help of a magnifying glass, she could read no more on that face. It was possessed of no mystery. Compared to the large color photograph of Samuel that she kept on the mantel in the parlor, with its generous smile that held nothing back, the snapshot in her hand was of a sick man who had known pain and expected more of it. He looked twenty years older than Samuel, although she knew they were the same age. This was taken before the operation, she decided.

But that he had sent it! Actually looked for and found the photograph, then put it in an envelope and *mailed* it. That heart is *working*, she thought. Hannah smiled and fixed herself a tuna-salad sandwich and a glass of milk.

She waited exactly two weeks—it wasn't easy—before she answered.

Dear Mr. Pope,
Thank you so much for the photo. I have put it in my scrapbook. My friend Ivy Lou, who is sort of an actuary, has calculated that your face occupies 2.1% of the picture and what with the peaked cap, you are a bit hard to make out. But, still. I like your backyard, is it? Are those azaleas on the right of the live oak you are leaning against? I have a live oak in my backyard too.

Sincerely yours,
Hannah Owen

Six weeks later, another letter arrived.

Dear Mrs. Owen,

My wife Inez will be in Little Rock visiting her parents on the weekend of October 20th. If you still want to come, I don't see why not, so long as you just stay for one hour. I will expect you at the house at ten o'clock Saturday morning. You know where it is, I'm sure.

Yours truly,
Henry Pope

"I wouldn't drive, if I were you," said Ivy Lou. "Not wound as tight as you are. Why you're as nervous as a bride. See if there's a bus." It was the first piece of Ivy Lou's advice Hannah thought she should take. She didn't trust herself to drive. Besides, she wanted the time to think, to prepare herself. Like a bride, she agreed, but she quickly shooed that notion out of her mind. There was an early-morning bus that got to Avery at nine-thirty, and the next day, before dawn, Hannah was on it. But once on the bus, she couldn't think, only reached up now and then to touch her right ear, which, when the bus stopped in Avery, would become a mollusc that would attach itself to the rock of Henry Pope's chest and cling through whatever crash of the sea.

▼   ▼   ▼

Number eight was one of a dozen identical single-family ranch houses that made up the dead end that was Orchard Road, only this one ennobled by the big live oak at the back, which fringed and softened the flat roof. At precisely ten o'clock Hannah unlatched the front gate and walked up to the door. Before she could ring the bell, the door opened halfway.

"Come in," he said, keeping himself out of sight until the door was closed behind her. The house was in darkness, every shade and blind drawn and shut. It had the same furtive, tense look she saw on the face of the man standing before her.

"No need to call attention," he said. "It would be hard to explain if anyone saw you come in." He was, she saw, a healthy man who looked even younger than she knew him to be. He had put on at least twenty pounds since that picture had been taken. His hair was light brown, almost blond and curly. He was wearing jeans and a white T-shirt.

He's nervous as a cat, thought Hannah, and that makes two of us.

Hannah followed him into a small room, a den furnished with a sofa, an upholstered easy chair, and a television set. One wall was lined with bookshelves. She guessed that he had spent his convalescence in this room.

"It's your show," he said. "How do you want me?" When she didn't answer, he reached up with both arms and pulled the T-shirt over his head.

"I suppose you want this off," he said. Then Hannah saw on his chest the pale violet stripe that marked the passage of her husband's heart into this man. She felt her pulse racing. She might faint.

"Well, it's your show," he said again. "How do you want to do this? Come on, let's just get it over with. One hour, you said."

"Best, I think, for you to lie down flat," she said. "I'll sit on the edge and lean over." She had gone over it so many times in her mind.

He lay down and slid a small pillow beneath his head, then shifted as far as he could to give her room to sit. When she did, he rose abruptly to his elbows.

"Where is your stethoscope?"

"I don't have a stethoscope."

"How are you going to listen to my heart without a stethoscope?"

"They didn't always have them," she said. "I'm going to listen with my ear." She gave her right ear two short taps. "I have very acute hearing," she added, because he looked dubious, as though he might call the whole thing off. But he didn't, just lay back down and stared straight up at the ceiling with his arms at his sides, as though he were still a patient at the hospital awaiting some painful procedure.

Then Hannah bent her head, turning toward the left, and lowered first to her elbows, then all the way, lowering her ear toward his left, his secret-sharing, nipple. When she touched his skin, she could feel him wince.

Oh, it was Samuel's heart, all right. She knew the minute she heard it. She could have picked it out of a thousand. It wasn't true that you couldn't tell one heart from another by the sound of it. This one was Sam's. Hadn't she listened to it just this way often enough? When they were lying in bed? Hadn't she listened with her head on his chest, just this way, and heard it slow down after they had made love? It was like a little secret that she knew about his body and it had always made her smile to think of the effect she had on him.

Hannah settled and gave herself up to the labor of listening. Closing her eyes, she drew herself down, down into that one sense of hearing, shedding sight and touch and all her other senses, peeling away everything that was not pure hearing until the entire rest of her body was an adjunct to her right ear and she was oblivious to whatever else might be in the world. She listened and received the deep regular beat, the emphatic *lub-dup, lub-dup* to which with all her own heart she surrendered. Almost at once, she felt a sense of comfort that she had not known in three years. She could have stayed there forever, bathed in the sound and touch of that heart. Thus she lay, until her ear and the chest of the man had fused into a single bridge of flesh across which marched, one after the other, in cadence, the parade of that mighty heart. Her own pulse quieted to match it beat for beat. And now it was no longer sound that entered and occupied her, but blood that flowed from one to the other, her own blood driven by the heart that lay just beneath the breast, whose slow rise and fall she rode as though it were a small boat at anchor in a tranquil sea, and she a huddled creature waiting to be born.

At last Hannah opened her eyes and raised her head. Never, never had she felt such a sense of consolation and happiness. Had it been a dream? Had she fallen asleep? It was a moment before she felt his arm about her shoulders. How long, she wondered, had she lain encircled and unaware? She looked up to see that he was smiling down at her. Angels must smile like that, she thought.

"You were trembling," he explained. "It was like holding a bird."

Gently, Hannah disengaged herself and stood, but listening still, cocking her ear for scraps of sound, echoes. And it seemed to her in the darkened room that light emanated from the naked torso of the man and that the chest upon which she had laid her head was a field of golden wheat in which, for this time, it had been given to her to go gleaning.

Henry Pope followed her to the door.

"Will you want to come again, Hannah?" he asked. How soft and low his voice as he uttered her name.

"No," said Hannah. "There will be no need." And she stepped out into the golden kingdom of October with the certainty that she had at last been retrieved from the shadows and set down once more upon the bright lip of her life. All the way home on the bus a residue of splendor sang in her ears.

PIPISTREL

pip-is-trelle, pip-is-trel (pip´ i strel´, pip´i strel´) *n*. [Fr. *pipistrelle*
< It. *pipistrello*, altered < OIt. *vispistrello* < L. *vespertilio*, bat <
vesper, evening: see VESPER] any of a genus (*Pipistrellus*) of
small bats that characteristically fly early in the evening: found
in N. America and in most of the Eastern Hemisphere

Lying awake in her bed, Ada heard the boy sigh and permitted a
glance inside herself. Had it really happened? She searched the
shadows for scraps of memory. Were it not for the evidence in the
next room, the boy's thin arms and legs strewn in the carelessness
of sleep, she might have doubted that eighteen years ago a young
man named Philip Schuster had come down to Schuylerville from
the high pastures beyond Sleeping Giant mountain, his sandy hair
combed back into two soft waves above a trustworthy smile, his
boots polished to the brightest black, and carrying into the house
that smell of cud, manure, and milk that ever since had the power
to reawaken instantly the whole of the buried past. From that first
Saturday night, he had made her feel *selected*. For his part, he told
her later, he had been beside himself with desire for her. For me!
she thought, amazed. And his was a desire entirely above ground,
a dumb, animal desire that he brought down from the hills every
Saturday and held up for her to see. Now and then, amid that
smile she saw a minute, serious glance upon her, as if only she had
the power to rescue him. Until—was it only six weeks later?—he

had fixed her with a gaze full of longing and told her he wanted to look after her from then on. Standing so close, she could feel the heat that radiated from the man's body, and swaying toward him, she let herself be lit by the conflagration. "You mean get married?" she asked. She had to be sure. She had flashed with excitement at the nakedness of it, his offer that she say yes or no to him while he waited in his misery and hope. Then she took in both of hers the hand he held out to her, turned it over to study the calluses on the cushions of his palm and the long lifeline that went almost up to his wrist. "Yes, I want to," she said into the glow that was his face, and heard his groan of jubilation as he drew her to him and pressed her head against his chest, where she inhaled the sweet clovery breath that emanated from it. Three months to the day after they had met, Ada and Philip Schuster left the First Presbyterian Church as man and wife and went to live on the farm beyond the mountain. And three months after that, he left for Korea, and that was that. Or almost that. For by the end of the year she was a mother and a widow. Philip, she named the boy, so as not to lose track. Long lifeline, indeed.

Ada rose and went to stand by his bed. Search as she would in the boy for his father—a curve of the lip, the lift of an eyebrow, the slow swelling of his features, like the rising of dough, that used to tell her soon he would make love to her—she could not find the least sign of him. What she saw instead was an ill-wrapped bundle of sticks that would not grow beyond four feet tall, with a pointed face as white as chalk and red watery eyes that, even in sleep, seemed to try to avoid the light. And, hovering over that face, the strange vacancy she was to spend the rest of her life trying to fathom. All at once, her son opened his eyes to see her standing over him. Ada smiled and stroked his head, not much bigger than a boxer's fist, the way one strokes a cat.

"Go back to sleep, Pippo," she said. A moment later, having given no sign that he had seen her, the boy turned on his side and closed his eyes. Ada felt her heart expand with love.

When he was four and started at his rocking back and forth (he would keep it up for hours), and he wasn't paying attention or talking except for "Mama" and "Pippo"—which was how he said Philip—she dressed him up in his good chinos and white shirt and took the bus to Albany, to the children's clinic.

"Autistic," said the doctor.

"What's that? Feeble-minded?"

"No. His brain is as good as yours or mine, only the circuits are all broken."

"Can it be fixed?"

"You have to accept it. You'd best put him somewhere nice with others like him and people to look after him."

"What caused it?"

"Nobody knows. It just happens."

"Come on, Pippo," she said then. "Let's go home."

"If it gets to be too much, let us know," said the nurse. "There's a place right here in Albany."

"No thanks," said Ada. And she meant it. That was thirteen years ago. In all those years he hadn't said any but those two words—*Mama* and *Pippo*. Other than that, little barks and chittering noises were what he made, and whimpers whenever he hurt himself. When he was happy, which was most of the time, he smiled and sort of sang, a long quavery singsong, up and down and on and on. To Ada he was the purest, sweetest thing God ever made. You're like an apple, she thought, looking at him, that's been picked too soon, but on purpose, to avoid the possibility of worms.

Oh, he could be stubborn, all right. There were things she couldn't get him to do. Wear his glasses, for one. No matter how she coaxed, or showed him how he could see better if he would, he wouldn't, but clawed them off as though they were burning hot. "All right," she said at last. "You don't have to. You will see what you will see."

At the children's clinic they had told her what she already knew, that he could draw better than anyone else his age. After she'd sold the farm, they'd moved to a small house a mile and a half outside of town, and over the years, new people had moved in and houses had been added to the outskirts, until one day Ada woke up to find herself living on the edge of town with neighbors and their children. And all through the years he had continued to draw, everything—trees, birds, roads, houses, the sky, the earth. Animals were his favorites—cows, sheep, goats, horses, and those pigs with each bristle slanted just so and the black crinkles about their eyes. Everything but people. He never once drew a human being. It was as if the whole world of his imagination did not contain one. He doesn't see us, Ada thought, for the vacancy around him. She couldn't keep him in paper, paint, and pencils. Once a month she'd send for supplies by mail order. A carton would arrive, and by the end of the month it would be used up. And every evening after supper, they'd sit together on the porch or by the stove and he'd show her his pictures. Sometimes he'd make five or six all of the same thing, a particular part of the path to the pond, a willow tree with a nesting bird, a mule cart, did it over and over until somehow he was satisfied.

"You're a perfectionist," she told him. When he gave her that sweet, dumb, blank look, she explained.

"It means you're persnickety. You've got to get it right." He must have drawn that willow tree a hundred times. Every chance she got, Ada brought him to the pond, where it leaned into the water. Sometimes he wouldn't draw, only sat by the edge of the water, gazing into it, and no matter how excited he had been, rocking or worse, banging his head on the wall, it turned him tranquil and dreaming.

"You know what I think?" she said. "I think you're a genius. Are you a genius? Come on and tell me."

After a while, he began to mix the colors himself, until he got what he wanted. He liked soft colors the best—browns, grays, yellows, ochers, and reds. Ada thought it was because they were easier on his eyes. He couldn't stand brightness in his pictures any more than he could in real life, when he could go about with his face scrunched up and his eyes squeezed almost shut to keep out the light, or walk in the yard with his hands over his eyes. You'd think he'd bump into things, but he never did. At the last moment, something would tell him there was a rock or a tree in his path and he'd turn aside just in time. Like a bat, thought Ada. He's like a bat that hears echoes of things and so doesn't collide with them.

All along, she had never stopped talking to him, saying whatever came to mind as though he were a normal person who would hear what she was saying and answer back. Oh, he could hear, all right, more and better than she could—far-off thunder, a train whistle, a flock of geese a mile high. It was as though his hearing made up for what he couldn't see. She'd watch him lift his head and cock his ear.

"What is it, Pippo? Is it thunder?" If he gave a little smile, that meant yes and she knew to take the clothes down off the line and throw the tarp over the woodpile. And sure enough, a couple of hours later, there'd be a storm. Mostly, though, he wouldn't answer, just sit on the floor with his narrow back to her, his shoulder blades outlined under his shirt like the winglets of some flightless bird. But it was not for her to say what got through and what didn't.

Pippo had another gift. Perfect aim. She had found this out when he was twelve. It was the way he picked up a pebble and threw. It was always *at* something, and he would hit it nine times out of ten.

"Let's go out and play," she said to him one day. "I'll set you up." She put a tin can on top of a fence post and watched him pick out the stone he wanted, just the right size and shape. How he walked up and down, back and forth, drawing a bead on that can, settling on the range. And not till he was good and ready would he throw. At last, *ping!* It was amazing, considering that she couldn't hit the side of the toolshed with a shovel. It wasn't play. She could see that. It was business. A year later she was tossing the can up in the air. He'd be off in a corner, quivering as he waited for her to release it, then back would go that skinny white arm and *ping!*

"You!" she laughed, and pulled him to her. "With your weak eyes. It's a grace," she told him. "A donation."

One Sunday in church, the preacher was telling about David and Goliath, how David chose five smooth stones out of the brook and went forth to meet Goliath. How he put his hand in his shepherd's bag and took from thence a stone, and "slang it and smote the Philistine so that he fell upon his face to the earth." All at once, Ada sat straight up in the pew and almost said it out loud: slingshot! As soon as she got home, she looked in the Sunday-school reader for the picture of David, then went rummaging. From a piece of old rawhide, she cut strips for the handles, then stitched them to a swatch of canvas for the pouch. The whole thing didn't take her more than an hour. When she held it up for him to see, and he didn't, she took him outside and swung it round and round over her head. Because he still looked puzzled, she put a pebble in the pouch and showed him again, watched his head circle to follow the path of her arm. When she let go of one of the cords and the pebble shot out, understanding flamed up in his eyes.

"There now," she said. "It's your turn."

It didn't take him more than an hour to figure out how to use it. In six months that boy could hit the tin can in midair no matter where she threw it, or how she tried to trick him by pretending to toss it one way and throwing it back over her shoulder at the last minute. How could he tell? She guessed that he figured it out from the way her arm moved and from the sound the can made as it flew into the air, a sound only he could hear. Then she decided that it was instinct and had nothing to do with air currents or acceleration or curvature. One day she took him for a picnic up on Sleeping Giant, and when she saw him knock a crow out of the air, she knew he could take care of himself if the time came. Ever afterward, she thought it was God telling her what to do that Sunday in church.

He loved her to pet him. Ada never knew when the notion would strike him; he'd come running up to her and throw his arms around her legs, imprisoning her until she dropped everything and took him, big as he was, on her lap, and he'd all but purr. Oh, he did want to be loved, and never once did she turn him down. She knew what it was to want loving and find there was none to be had. Later, she thanked God for every single time she had held that boy in her arms and kissed him.

But as time went on, what was enough for her would not appease the world. There came the day when she heard a commotion out in the yard and looked out to see two big boys laughing and roaring outside the fence. One of them—she thought it was Lloyd Baskin's son—picked up a stone and threw it at Pippo, and then the other boy did the same. She saw Pippo get up from where he was squatting and scamper about the yard, flapping his arms and chittering at the fun, because neither of the stones had hit him. She knew that at this distance he could have hit them every time. But all at once, there was another stone, which hit him in the center of his forehead, and he fell down, bleeding. By the time she got to him, the big boys had run off. She knelt and turned him over into her lap, and saw his thin white face streaming blood.

"It's all right," she said. "All right." But he didn't so much as grasp her hand when she took his. Just lay there bleeding and blinking his little red eyes. Ada did what she knew, scooped him up—he weighed no more than seventy pounds—and carried him into the house and washed his wound and pressed it until it stopped bleeding, and she kissed and kissed him over and over. At that moment, if she could, she would have stuffed him back into her womb to keep him safe. Hours went by as she rocked him in her arms, her tears falling on his cheeks, and Mary, Mother of

God, couldn't have felt worse with crucified Jesus on her lap. And
Ada saw that over his countenance a veil had dropped. She could
feel him falling away from her in a wail, but no sound came. The
bright time is over, she said to herself. But it wasn't the wound in
his forehead that told her, so much as the bloodless white wound
that was his face. He had tasted of the fruit of the world, reached
out for it with his heart full of joy, and found it bitter as the
apples of Sodom. He wouldn't try again. Next morning, looking
down at the purple dent in his forehead with the clotted blood
around it, she told him:

"Don't you worry. I'll go outside with you from now on."

It was only weeks later that there was more trouble. It was a
rainy day, but she had let him out anyway in his black raincoat.

"I'll be right out in a minute," she said. "You'll be all right."

And then: "Pippo, you're batty," she heard one of them call
out; it was the same two boys and now two girls.

"Be a bat, Pippo," said another. All at once, from beyond the
fence came a howl of pain. Pippo was standing in the middle of
the yard, swinging the slingshot. He let fly another stone, and she
heard another yelp behind the fence. She was out the door in a
flash, just in time to see a third stone go sailing, the boys and girls
running off, roaring, one holding his arm. Ada threw herself on
Pippo, grabbing his arm so hard he whimpered.

"Here you, Pippo," she said, and shook him hard. "Don't, I
said. Don't you ever do that again." She had never spoken to him
like that, so harshly. "Because if you do, I'll take it away from
you and you'll never see it again." When he raised his head to
look at her, something wild and yellow blazed up in his eyes, then
died down. It's fury, she thought. He's mad enough to bite me.
The one time that he acted like a man, defending himself, she had
stopped him. She held out her arm to his teeth.

"Bite me," she said. "Go ahead and bite me. I know you want
to." And I want you to, she thought. Just for a moment, his lips
drew back and quivered. But he didn't bite her, just sort of gave,

went limp and still. Ada put her arm around him and drew him into the house.

It wasn't an hour later that Lloyd Baskin and two other men were at her door.

"He's dangerous, Ada. Wild. You've got to put him away." The hate in their eyes, the desire for revenge. It frightened her and she could not conceal her fear.

"The idea! Letting that crazy little geek have a slingshot when you know he's got the Devil's own eye. Get him out of here."

"I'll never do that," she said. "Never."

"Whatever happens, then, will be your fault." Please, she wanted to say, please leave us alone. She would have dropped to her knees and kissed the hem of Lloyd Baskin's garment, if she had to. Inside, she knew the boy was listening, still wearing his black raincoat.

It wasn't the same after that. For one thing, he stopped coming to her for her caresses. When she captured him on her lap, he would let her, but that was all. The need had become all hers. And there were no more smiles, only that look of erasure.

"You've got to forget about it," she told him. "Some boys are like that out there, some aren't." And once, she found herself wondering whether she ought to have listened to that doctor and put him away with others of his kind. But only once and never again. And all the while, Ada knew that something was coming, something terrible that she would have to face. She felt it ticking in her ear.

▼   ▼   ▼

It was eight o'clock on the morning of the first day of June. Pippo was still asleep. She opened the refrigerator to take out the milk, and found there wasn't any. Ada wondered whether she had time to get to the market and back before he woke up. She opened the door to his room. Yes, he was sleeping. Deeply, from his slow, even breathing. She closed the door and left the house. The walk there and back wouldn't take more than twenty minutes if she hurried. Already, it was hot. Her head drummed with sunshine. Coming back, she saw that the front door was open, and she knew. She raced through the house, calling out for him, looking in the closets and out in the yard. But all the while, she knew that he was gone.

Still carrying the bottle of milk, she ran down the path to the pond, crying his name, searching the sky for clues. That afternoon, they organized search parties, fanned out in all directions. He couldn't have gotten far, they told her. Not that half-pint. But Ada knew otherwise. With what was calling out to him or driving him away, he could have gone to China. At nightfall, when there had been no sign of him, they quit for the day. Don't you worry, Ada, they said. He'll come back with his tail between his legs as soon as he's hungry. Tail? she thought. And she might have laughed, if her heart weren't breaking. All night, she prowled the house. Had he left her a sign? But she found nothing, only that he had taken the tackle box with his paints, brushes, charcoal sticks. And his slingshot.

For a week they searched the woods, dragged the pond. A police helicopter rattled back and forth over the house. The sheriff came.

"Give it up, Ada. We're quitting. There's no place we haven't looked. He can't still be alive, not with everything hungry that's prowling out there, and him with no more strength than a newborn chicken, and the little bit of sense he had. Something has taken him by now—a bear, dogs, crows. He's gone. Give it up." But she couldn't give it up. As the weeks went by she could not keep her hands off the thought of him. Time and again she took him who was not there onto her lap, old as he was, and hugged him and sang into his ear until he laughed and scratched it for the tickling.

One day she met Lloyd Baskin on the street.

"It don't look good," he said. She thought he didn't mind letting her know. Well, maybe, but Ada wasn't convinced. And all that day and night she debated with Lloyd Baskin in her mind. When you were like Pippo, you didn't need to get any stronger or bigger or older to survive. You only had to know what was your range, and stay inside it. Besides, whatever instincts for survival he was going to get, he already had. He was born with them. Unless you were talking about human beings, survival wasn't at all a matter of intelligence or wit or even very much experience. It had to do with animal cunning, which is another way of saying intuition, something that seemed to her situated in the nerves and muscles, not the brain. As for being big and strong, that might be more of a handicap than anything. A sparrow didn't want to be big and strong, or a mouse. It wanted to be small and quick, and that's what Pippo was.

"We'll see," she said to Lloyd Baskin. Besides, Pippo had his slingshot and could hit a crow taking off from a corn patch three out of four times. Maybe there's not much behind it, but he's got an eye up front, where it counts, she thought. Ada had heard about wild boys who were found in the forest after years of living like animals on roots, nuts, and small creatures. Hadn't they managed to survive? He's got all the sense he needs to get himself home. He just doesn't want to come home yet.

But now it was October, four months since he'd gone. For four months she had waited and watched; from behind the curtains, from the farthest edges of the pond, from the woods on the outskirts of the village. She had worn herself out watching. She had walked the streets calling his name out loud and in her heart, hunted in the grass for his footsteps, sniffed the trunks of trees, burned herself at the stove, forgotten to eat, and she who did not stumble, stumbled. And every night she lay herself down like ashes after the fire. She couldn't take it anymore. It was eating her up alive. Hope was worse than finality. Hell was better than limbo. Ada decided to clean out his room.

After the first week, she hadn't gone in there, just couldn't. But now it was time. Without looking to right or left, she marched straight to the closet. The sight of his clothes made her dizzy but she gripped herself hard and started taking down the hangers, carrying things to the bed. Back and forth three times, before she saw, tacked up on the wall behind the clothes rack, a painting she hadn't seen before. He always showed her his paintings, but she hadn't seen this one. Tacked up on the wall, but hidden behind the clothes. She had to wonder.

Ada took the picture down and brought it into the light. He'd used a page from his sketchbook. The picture showed Sleeping Giant in charcoal and watercolors. There was the old man of the mountain, lying on his back, half sunken into or half emerging from the earth. Arms at his sides, that blank Indian face shut in on itself, only here smudged with the shadow of a passing cloud, hands and feet hairy with shrubbery, the bare torso strewn with tawny boulders. Just as she had known it all her life, and Pippo too, from the many times they had gone there. And the whole of the mountain not muted, but yellow and hot with bright sunshine, everything casting a shadow. Her eyes swept across the length of the paper and back, from top to bottom, when, as if a finger had pointed, her gaze was caught and held at the black thumbnail, no more than an eighth of an inch across, near the bottom of the painting. And even that half hidden in tall weeds. Anyone could have missed it. Black, she thought. A black thumbnail? Perhaps it was a jot of charcoal he had meant to fill in, only forgot. No, it was black paint, a dab of it. Besides, he never forgot in his painting. Without reason in much else, he had a reason for every speck and line he drew. And Ada peered and peered until the black thumbnail softened and gave way so that she was looking through it, into a place behind that you could enter, a hole. "The cave," she said out loud.

Ada took off her apron, put a flashlight in her pocket, and left the house. A moment later, she returned, put three plums in her pocket, and left again. Already the sun was three quarters down the sky. It would be dark by the time she got there. It took an hour and a half to reach the foot of Sleeping Giant, then another thirty minutes up the steep path choked with briers. All the way, she berated herself for not finding it before, the message that maybe he had left for her and meant her to find, not to bring him home, but only that she should know. At the giant's hand, she stepped off the path into the underbrush. Not twenty paces in, she stopped, turned in a half circle, and there it was, partially obscured by small gray bushes that leaned across the entrance. The cave! The monstrous cave. She would stand it. She would have to. She stared at the mouth of the cave for a long while, inhaling the sour air that came from it, and she shivered with a premonition that went deep, deeper than sorrow. *No hope*, it seemed to say. *There is no hope.*

Ada stepped into the mouth of the cave, counted her steps to ten, then stopped, waiting for her eyes to accommodate to the darkness. Another ten paces, one blind foot fumbling after the other, her arms outstretched, parting the darkness like a swimmer parting water. Here the passageway was so narrow that she could reach out and touch the sweating walls; there, it broadened and she was left unmoored. The darkness swirled with violent shapes. All at once, fear, which she had not yet felt, slammed into her with an impact that made her stagger. Not of the darkness or whatever else was in it, but of something that dropped to her neck, then skittered off. She prayed for the strength she would need if she found him lying sprawled and lifeless. Or if she stumbled onto him with her foot. Spare me that, she cried to herself. At least not that. With trembling hands, she flicked on the flashlight she had not dared to use because of what she might see, and followed the beam to the wall of the cave. She reached out, palming the slime. She sprayed the light to the high vault, then down at the floor, where she saw, almost at her feet, something pale and gleaming. Bending closer, she drilled it with the light. Her heart hammered against her ribs. A skull! She could make out the jaw, a row of teeth. No, it was too small, and the teeth were those of an animal, a raccoon, perhaps. She touched it with her shoe, tapped it. Nearby there were other bones. A rib, the long bone of a leg, a scattering of dark fur, some feathers. But she could not bring herself to go deeper. Ada backed toward the mouth of the cave, guarding herself with the cone of light until she stood in the entrance. Then she remembered the plums, stepped back inside, and set them down just inside the opening.

When she left the cave, it was raining. On the way down the path she was watched carefully by a doe and her fawn. How they turned their narrow heads and pointed their ears as she passed! All the way home, in her mind, she saw him running into that cave for the first time, his black hair sticking out at his temples, accompanied only by his own terror, which she hoped had not gone inside with him, but had stayed out in the world from which he had run. So long as he stayed in that cave, he was safe. He had found the one place where he could live. From the bones and feathers, she guessed that he had already used his slingshot. Now he had all the darkness he could wish for, and no bright sun to burn his eyes. When she thought about it, the cave wasn't completely dark. The walls glowed with their own light, like phosphorus. After a while, you could see a bit, even without the flashlight. It was as dark as that when her front porch put its long arms around her and drew her inside the house.

The next day, Ada slept until noon. She decided to wait until late afternoon; there was less chance of being seen. At three o'clock, she filled a pint bottle with soup, buttered two slices of bread, and put it all in a paper bag. She unpacked a box of paint tubes that had come after he had gone, stuffed half a dozen in her pockets, tested the flashlight to make sure it was working, and set out for Sleeping Giant. It was five-thirty when she got there. Sunset, she saw, was preparing in the west. Without hesitation, she entered the cave, turned on the light, and edged slowly along the wall. The first thing she noticed was that the plums weren't where she had placed them. So that's it, she thought, and set down the bag of bread and soup.

"Pippo!" she called softly and heard her voice being swallowed by the cave. "Pippo!" She pressed her hand against the wall as if to invoke him from the stone. At twenty steps, the cave took a sharp turn. At thirty, she had to stoop low to get beneath a projection of rock. At fifty, she paused and listened to a tiny sound that grew suddenly, then died an instant later. Something slunk against her legs. When she looked down, there was nothing. When she looked up again, she saw on the wall the painted outline of a small hand. Ada advanced slowly. Another ten steps, another hand. And another. Here the cave narrowed to a cone, so that she had to go sideways and bend double. A dead end, she thought. He's not here. He's gone. Tears of disappointment ran down her face. She would leave—there was no more she could do.

But, look! Here was yet another hand, this one lower on the wall, at the level of her knees. Not pointing, but all the same, she thought, directing her gaze downward. Ada bent to see an opening in the rock, at ground level. It was no more than a foot and a half across, maybe two. The air coming from it was fetid and damp. She knelt down and lowered her head to peer in, but only the long beam of her flashlight was visible in the blackness. It was too small for her to crawl through. Ada flicked off the light and stood there in the dark. A greenish pallor seemed to float toward her from the stone walls.

The next day, Ada began her fast. I'm too fat, she thought. I can't get through, but soon I will, she insisted to some imagined adversary. Don't you worry, I will. It would be bread and water from then on. And it almost was. So help her, she didn't want a mouthful of anything else. It would have gagged her. Every afternoon she set out carrying a basket with the day's food, the flashlight, some painting supplies, a jackknife. Now and then, she'd stoop to pick up a stone that was the right size for the slingshot.

Without flinching now, she entered the great cave, where by day all the world's darkness seemed to crowd itself, massive and dense, until, with dusk, it seeped out to cover the earth once more. Once inside, her feet grew subtle as an animal's, committing the cave to memory. Now, without the flashlight, she could tell just when the cave took that sharp turn, where she had to bend down to keep from hitting her head. Now and then, she called out his name: "Pippo! Pippo!" But she knew he wouldn't answer or make a sign—except that whatever she put down in the entrance was gone the next morning. Something was working, something fragile that she knew she mustn't scare away.

Already her fear of the darkness was no longer absolute. She half liked it; half not. There was something sensual about it that was missing in broad daylight. She could almost feel her pupils dilating to take it in, willing herself to become a piece of the darkness. In a certain way, she could see why he hid from the sun. At the end of three weeks, Ada's clothes swam off her shoulders. She was two notches slimmer at the waist. Another week, and she would be ready to try. It would be tight, but she would have to see.

▼   ▼   ▼

Ada had arrived at the cave at dusk, her usual time, and had made her way inward some forty paces, about halfway to the tunnel, when something told her that the air was full of silent wings, beating. All around her head she heard a whisper, whisper, tiny squeaks. Panting like a dog, she pressed her back against the wall of the cave. Something flickered at her throat. By the time she had raised her hand to brush it off, it had gone, leaving an unclean sensation on her skin. Something else struck her softly on the chest, then on the fingers. In the pale green glow, the roof rolled like something brought to a boil. Now and then a wave swept across it, shaking free fragments of itself to swing like censers. A steady rain of droppings pelted her. The smell of ammonia choked. All at once, the whole ceiling began to billow like a tent come loose from its peggings. In a moment it would collapse. Ada could not hold in her terror, but wailed, and raised her arms against whatever was coming down upon her, forced shut her lips lest she find her mouth filled with something furry, stiff hairs on her tongue. And she forced herself to remain still, to just stand beneath that heaving roof, letting the swarm pass over and around her, buffeting, glancing off. Once, she felt a fluttering inside her chest. It was as though a bat had slipped between her ribs. If she could only stay there and bear it, and not give in to what was coiled tight inside her and ready to lay her screaming on the ground. If she could get through this, she would never be afraid again.

At last it was over. The cave had disgorged its colony for the night's feeding. Ada inhaled deeply and pulled the sudden quiet of the cave into her lungs, stilling herself with it after what had boiled all about her, what had, on its surge to the outside, swept along with it all of her resolve. Hollow and exhausted, she staggered from the cave. No, she thought, I cannot. Not today. She would try tomorrow.

▼   ▼   ▼

The next day, at noon, Ada was still lying in bed, husbanding her strength for what was to come. Now and then, she slept. Hours later she was aroused by a commotion outside. There was the shouting of men, the sound of running feet, a truck started up urgently. Then more shouting as the truck pulled away.

"Where?"

"One of the caves at Sleeping Giant."

"What was it doing?"

"Squatting in front, skinning something."

"A white man. Big, the kids said, with wild staring eyes, all dressed in black rags. Soon as he saw the kids, he ran into the cave."

"We'll follow you."

Ada ran to the window in time to see the last of the truck. There were three men in it and the barrel of a shotgun rested on its window ledge. That would be Lloyd Baskin. She struggled not to faint, while gold lights came and went behind her eyelids and the pictures on the walls shook as if to fall off. She dressed and ran out of the house. If she took the path by the pond, they wouldn't see her.

Ada ran until she couldn't anymore, then walked, then ran again. At the base of the mountain, she saw where they had left the truck. But they hadn't known the way from there, not the way she did, so that when she came up, it was in time to see the back of a man disappearing into the mouth of the cave. Ada trembled. A moment later, she had slipped through the hole. In the invisibility it bestowed on her, she grew calm. Not more than ten paces ahead, she saw the beams of their searchlights jerking from side to side. When all at once they halted, she knew that it was at the debris of bones. She crept closer to hear. She knew that he could hear them too, that somewhere in the cave he was staring into the darkness and listening.

"Stay close."

"Where are you, Buddy?"

"You never know what it's got to throw at us."

"Watch out! Goddammit." In the torchlight, the faces of the men were the color of butcher's meat. How could they not know she was there? Her heart was as loud to her as a bass drum, and she tried to still it with her hand. Then, a voice from which all the bravery had gone:

"Maybe we should quit for now, Lloyd. Come back in the morning, now we know where he's hiding. It'll be dark outside in a while."

"You think so?"

They're afraid, she thought. She saw them huddling together. Why, she could see right through them, as though they were glass, see their fear. And then she feared them all the more. For she remembered something that happened years ago when she and Philip were living on the farm, before Pippo. Philip had gone up to the pasture and she was alone, in the barnyard, when two huge sows began fighting. They had been scared by the boar in the neighboring pen, which had, somehow, tossed a stone over the railing. She had never seen anything like it. The great tusks thrusting into each other, the hidden teeth burrowing and clamping. The screams, the blood, until they both lay mangled and dead. Ada remembered, and trembled.

She grew crafty. She, who had challenged the darkness again and again, would call upon it now to befriend her. Lifting her eyes and her arms to it, she prayed for twilight and its creatures to stream forth and darken the sky, for the exodus of the bats, which was like an echo of the setting sun. Come, Night! she all but hollered. They'll never stand it, she thought. Not the way she'd had to and would again, gladly. Her mind was a deep well of scorn as she stood there, her arms raised like a witch summoning up spirits and calling out to the vast horde to come down upon them.

But the men had not turned back; they were picking their way forward. Already they had come to the place where the cave angled to the right. A little farther and they would be at the tunnel into which, day and night, for weeks, she had dispatched her soul. Up ahead, she heard voices overlapping, echoing, but full now of the hisses and coughs of trepidation.

"Phew! It stinks here. Batshit."

"Watch your step! What's this? It stops here. Far as she goes."

"Unless we've missed a turnoff. What now?"

"Back, I guess. There's no place else to go. Whatever it was, or wasn't, has gone." Ada held her breath. They hadn't seen it. But just then:

"Here you go! An opening. Look."

"Where?"

"Down near the ground. Looks like a tunnel of some kind, narrow, though, about a foot and a half around, maybe four feet long."

"What do you see? Anything?"

"Nothin'. Empty space."

"Hey you! Come out of there or we'll block it up."

"Yeah, Lloyd. We better block it up." They were torn between the desire to turn and run and the desire to see him, to encircle and goad.

"Let's smoke him out. Throw the canister in." Ada saw the shadow of an upraised arm.

"Stop!" It was her own voice, imperious, as she had never heard it. The beams of light jumped like fish, then swung toward the sound of her voice. She let them come, let them seek her out, travel over her body to her face and stop there, blinding her. She stared straight into them.

"What the hell! Who?"

"Ada! What the hell!"

"I can get through," she said quietly.

"No you don't. Keep out of this, Ada. Now you're here, we can't send you back. But stay the hell out of the way. If you think it's your boy . . ." She headed straight into the converged beams of light, took them full on her breast. Then reached for one of the flashlights. It came free from the hand that held it—willingly, she thought.

"Let her do it, Lloyd. If she can get in, she can damn well get out." Ada was already on her knees in front of the opening, then flat, her thin arms stretched in front. She let go of the flashlight and began scrabbling in the muddy floor. It was tight. For the first foot, there was hope; she clawed and toed her way for several inches, flicked the flashlight ahead with the backs of her fingers. At that point the passage narrowed. The back of her head hit against rock. Pebbly mud slid between her lips. Her shoulders wedged, scraped; more pushing with her toes. Another inch of progress. All at once, her strength left her, and she lay exhausted. Her chest, heaving, strained against the floor. She was clamped in a vise, had swollen to fill it. How could she have thought herself able to do it? Behind her, the voices of the men.

"You makin' it, Ada?" She forced down panic. Expelling all the air from her lungs, she sank her fingers into the stone floor, pushed with her feet. Her shoulders were throbbing with pain, something warm running down from her head. Then, bursting through the narrows, her shoulders spilling out into space. Kicking, pushing with her freed arms, until she was in. She had done it. A place so cool and damp and still, a tomb. No current of air. She stood shakily, reached up to touch her throbbing shoulder, felt the blood on her hand. Now she groped for the flashlight, flicked it on, and turned the beam in a slow, tentative circle. The floor was covered with silt. In the absolute humidity she was breathless. Within minutes she was dripping with the cold condensation. The walls of the chamber were a soft sandy color. At one place, water ran slowly down, screening it darkly. Spectral little beasts—white beetles, crayfish, and pink salamanders scurried out of range of the light. A recess in the wall coned down into a kind of passageway. She followed it, stooping low, stepping through shallow pools into which small insects plopped.

"Pippo!" she said softly. "Pippo, it's me. Don't be afraid. Please, Pippo, if you are here, let me know." There was no sound other than her own voice. "Pippo!" she called louder, and heard the name come echoing back to her. She must not let the men hear. All at once, her mind filled with the knowledge of his presence. He was here. She knew it. Her heart leaped and volleyed; she was panting. Ada let the light rove the walls, moving it upward little by little. All at once, it jumped in her hand. At one corner of the circle of light, something large and black hovered high, near the ceiling. Perhaps she thought rather than saw it? Holding the light with both hands to steady it, she brought whatever it might be into view.

He was hanging from what must be a narrow ridge, clinging with his fingers. His arms and legs, like sticks, emerged from a tatter of black rags. In the darkness of the cave, his skin was milk-white. The sinews stood out like rods with the effort of clinging. A tangle of black hair framed a face behind which the skull threatened to pop through.

"Pippo," she whispered. "Come down here to me. I won't hurt you. Oh, how I've missed you and worried. Come down." She came closer until she could see the droplets of moisture caught in the cloud of his hair. They glistened as he turned his head to stare down behind him. The little muscles around his nose and mouth twitched. His eyes, no longer red and watery, but dry and white, seemed to reach for her like suckers. The sight of him calmed her. The violent fluttering of her heart slowed. She stepped closer until she was just below him, then raised her hand. The dead-white eyes never left her.

"Take my hand," she said. "Touch me." Even on tiptoe she could not reach him. He made not the smallest movement, but clung motionless to whatever small crevice or jutting he had grasped. It was as though he were speaking to her for the first time. Let me be—he said it to her with his eyes, white as picked lilies. Let me stay—he begged her with his scrabbling fingers. If you take me out, I will die.

From far above, she heard the men calling, their words echoing.

"Ada! Get back here. You come back here right now-ow-ow."

"I'm coming . . . there's nobody here." She turned back to the boy. "Tomorrow," she whispered. "Tomorrow."

Then loudly, over her shoulder, she called out, "I'm coming."

The squeeze through the canal seemed to her not half so hard as before, as though the cave itself were not anxious to retain her. Once through, she stood up. From the other side of the tunnel came a low moan as of air entering an unseen cleft.

"It's empty," she told the men. "There's no one there."

"It's about time, damn you, Ada. We had half a mind to leave you here to rot. Jesus! You're covered with blood."

"Those kids must have made it up."

"Let's get out of here. Those kids are in for one hell of a licking." Ada submitted passively, followed them as they hurried each other along. They couldn't wait to get out. A queer sensation flooded her. It was, she thought, something like the happiness of the outlaw for whom eternal flight was preferable to a life as a law-abiding citizen.

"Tomorrow," she whispered to herself. "Tomorrow."

They were no more than fifty steps from the entrance when Ada felt it coming. Felt the entire cave turn over in its sleep, the air thrilling with wings. She willed her body to shut down, to still itself until she was no more than another palpitation in the dark disquiet. And she stood, arms akimbo, in the teeth of the onslaught, fearless and grateful, receiving the fluttering horde, drawing them upon her arms like sleeves, while, ahead, she saw the men flailing about, stamping, yelling in their terror, staggering into one another. Through minutes of it she stood, relishing the plague she had brought down upon their heads to which only she was immune. And she marveled at the power of love that drives even the fear of death out of the heart. "Jesus!" they screamed. And "Jesus!" When it had passed, she saw them gather themselves up, whipped, and leave the cave once and for all. They would not return.

Ada waited until she heard the truck start up and drive off before she, too, stepped from the cave. It was almost midnight when she opened the door of her house, her shoulders throbbing where the stone of the passageway had bitten in, her fingertips stinging raw from the scrabbling to which she had set them. That night she did not go to bed, but sat in the chair rocking, rocking, and thinking of his white forehead boring through the tunnel and of that chamber all about and above her with everything that was alive and quivering in its high reaches. At precisely five o'clock the next afternoon, she rose and washed herself with water from the china pitcher, thrusting her head into the bowl of cold water again and again until she felt clean and hard and sharp. When she left the house, she was carrying only the kerosene lamp and a box of matches. During the whole of that day she had made only one decision—to take a kerosene lantern. A flashlight, she decided, would not do for a chamber what it would a passageway.

▼   ▼   ▼

The small black eye of the channel gazed gravely up at her. She knelt, then lay down on the slimy floor, her arms stretched forward. She had thrust the lamp on ahead as far as she could. Raking with her fingers, she pulled herself forward, using her hips and knees until once again she lay in the clutch of stone. Then, bending her ankles, she pushed with her toes. It was slow; minutes went by seemingly without a bit of progress. The channel bit into her head, her arms. She felt a hard pressure on her chest. For one moment, she felt a wave of nausea, but she fought it down, and alternated her thrusts with deep exhalations. When she felt the sudden little give, and felt the rock cut deeply into her flesh, she heard herself moan.

Now her head was free and gasping into space. A push, a clawing at nothing, a tiny twist. One shoulder through. Then the other, then gathering her chest, trunk, abdomen, and legs behind her like the segments of a worm, she flung what was left of her torn body through into freedom. She stood, groped for the lamp, touched a match to the wick, and held it aloft. She stepped toward the wall where she had seen him suspended the day before. Back and forth, up and down, she swung the lantern. He was not there. Only, high on the wall, near the recess leading to the next corridor, the print of his hand. She went toward the niche, and stooped to enter the next chamber.

Ada found herself in a high-domed room with inward sloping walls. She stepped to the center of the room and raised the lantern; she gasped. Riding across the walls was a frieze of many cattle, their curved horns intersecting, tails describing patterns. Here a bull jumped, while another lowered its horns. There, a donkey waggled its ears. Horses reared. Trees arched near the ceiling, with bats in full fight or hanging like leaves. And the colors—ocher, brown, reddish brown, yellow, gray—his colors. Each figure etched into the wall with something sharp, a rock, she guessed, then outlined in charcoal and painted. She saw how he had used the curves and hollows of the walls to give the animals movement, to make them gallop or pant. The flickering of the lantern gave flight to the bats. Ada had the feeling that she was standing on a great plain where herds were galloping and swirling about her. She seemed to hear their lowing, the shrieking of birds, the thudding of prehistoric hooves, and though she could neither name nor place them, memories were being stirred somewhere deep within her.

It is the creation of the world I am beholding, she thought. But a world not meant to be seen. Why? It was just the urge to make it, she thought. Gazing about her, Ada felt that she could at last see into the heart of the boy, which had always been hidden from her. Here it was, illuminated. She walked the circumference of the chamber, her lamp held high, searching the walls for him. But he was not there. She would go home, then. She had to think. No one could tell her what to do. Ada had turned to leave the chamber when her foot touched something soft, and she stumbled, almost fell. She lowered the lamp to see his foot, thin and white, the delicate toes. He lay where he had fallen, his moth-white face bent backward, too far back, and twisted on his neck. The blinding white stripe of his teeth, his wrinkled nose, the eyes, pale and staring.

In the midst of that glory of herds, that flight of birds, all of his exquisite seed sown there in the darkness, Ada rejoiced in the full-grown manhood that at last he had won. She looked down again at the thin twisted neck, the narrow bloody paws with their tiny talons, the cracked head pasted to the floor of the cave with black blood. Then, all about his head and body, she saw pulsating a halo of pale beetles, crayfish, salamanders, scurrying at his face, his fingers, and her grief welled up anew. Weeping, she set down the lamp, knelt, and wiped her hands again and again across the floor of the cave, gathering the wet silt into her palms, then turned to smear him—cheek, brow, hands, and feet—with the slimy earth. Then Ada lay down beside him, settled herself, and watched the waning lamplight enliven the herds until, at last, the flame died down, blazed up, died down, and went out.

LINDOW MAN

It was an evening in mid-March, still winter in New Haven, where, in a house at the edge of the university, Frederick Nolan sat alone in his study. A small fire burned in the grate and a single lamp behind his chair produced a parabola of orange light. Otherwise the house was dark and silent. A night walker glancing in the window might have noticed a neglected interior, muted with dust, smoke, and shadows, in which the man himself was as motionless as one of those dry desert creatures, a toad perhaps, or a lizard that takes on the subdued coloration of its background in order not to be seen.

Idly, Nolan's unfocused gaze fell to the few papers and letters on the desk before him. He had meant to read none of them. But, in the immobility in which he was cloaked, one envelope offered itself to his hand. He saw that it was postmarked London, England, and had been mailed more than a month before. The return address told him that it was from Adam Foulkes, a former colleague with whom he had collaborated in writing some archaeological papers. They had worked together in the field often, and had, for a time, been friends. Mechanically, Nolan slit open the envelope and began to read:

Dear Nolan,
Here is a story that will amuse you. [It was just like Foulkes to plunge right in.] In the parish of Mobberley, on the outskirts of Wilmslow,

Cheshire, lies the bog of Lindow Moss. Men work there harvesting peat. Mostly, they use triangular shovels as in the old days, but now, too, there is a machine, a sort of tractor with a large blade to slice strips of peat from the bog. The machine is called a HY-MAC. The strips of peat are stacked to dry for six months, then brought by narrow-gauge railroad to a station, where workers examine the trays of peat for impurities—stones, logs, whatever. One day in May of 1983, a worker at the station retrieved from the peat something round. It was too light for a rock. A burst football, he thought. Perhaps he tossed it playfully to his co-worker, who threw it aside. After a few days, the discarded object was noticed to be producing an unpleasant odor. Reexamination revealed that here was no burst football but a human head, a woman's, with skin and muscles, black hair, and one (the left) eyeball and inside, a yellowish-green paste that had been the brain. The police were called in.

Now it happened that in a bungalow adjacent to the bog there lived a man who was under suspicion of having, years ago, murdered his wife, of having then dismembered her body and buried the parts in his garden. Of course, the man denied having done so. Dig how they would over the months of the investigation, the police could find not the least portion of her corpse. But now, there was this head! Imagine, if you will, Nolan, the police inspector listening yet again to the man's emphatic denial of the crime. Imagine him then slowly unwrapping the head, all the while scrutinizing the other for the least twitch of surprise. On his own face, the tiniest snake of a smile. No need. One glance at the head of the woman, and the man broke and confessed to the murder, for which he was in short order committed to prison. Fifty years ago that would have been that, but now the head was shipped off to the police laboratory in Oxford. Carbon dating was carried out. The head was found to have lived A.D. 200, give or take eighty years.

Nor is that all. One year later, in August of 1984, another worker, scanning the peat as it moved slowly before him on the railway, pulled out a sizable tree branch and threw it aside. The peat fell away from the branch and—what was this? The "branch" was nonesuch, but a human leg, perfectly preserved. Again, the police were summoned, but now also the scientists—an archaeologist, an anatomist, a paleobiologist, all the rest of our tribe. A search was made for the remainder of the body. It was no long time before what they were seeking was found. Yards from the original site, a flap of skin, like a dorsal fin, was seen to be protruding from the surface of the bog. The excavation, en bloc, including the cocoon of peat in which it lay, yielded the preserved body of a man. Or the rest of it, minus, of course, that heraldic leg. He was naked, wearing only a cord of rawhide right about his neck. A twig used for twisting was wedged between the neck of the man and the cord. A large wound was present in the abdomen from which the viscera protruded. Once again to Oxford and the laboratory. He had lived, it was made known, in the year 550 B.C.

The specimen, now preserved (not freeze-dried as you might expect, but treated by the old Danish method), was transported to the British Museum, where it has been on permanent exhibit. It has proved immensely popular. Schoolchildren are brought by the busload to file by the glass case mounted on a pedestal, where the man lies in conditions of controlled temperature and humidity. Scientists, secretaries on their lunch hours, housewives, and clerks have visited. And from all over England, thousands of the curious have made the pilgrimage to this room. Pete Marsh is the name he has been given by the curator, who offered the remark that, upon entering the room, people will invariably lower their voices or stop talking altogether. The man himself seems to provoke this subdued response. . . .

Nolan read no further, letting the letter slip from his fingers. For a long time he sat still in the orange lamplight, then reached for a paper and pen.

Dear Foulkes,
Would you be good enough to arrange indefinite lodgings for me as close to Lindow Moss as possible? Simplest is best. I will be arriving on the first of April.

Yours,
Frederick Nolan

As he could not have said why he had read that one of all the letters, so Nolan could not have explained his sudden determination to go to Lindow Moss. It had nothing to do with the reawakening of his scientific curiosity, dormant these ten years since the death of his wife. It seemed rather a journey he had been called upon to make in accordance with a will other than his own. Something to do with the strange buried man and his recovery from the bog; something to do with murder.

Nolan was fifty-two at the time of his reading of the events at Lindow Moss. After the death of his wife, he had abruptly resigned his position on the archaeology faculty, closed his laboratory, and retired behind what his puzzled colleagues liked to think of as a quiet, unmolested door. In fact, Nolan had entered into a state of almost complete reclusiveness that was less a peaceful retirement than a kind of hibernation marked by silence and lethargy. For the most part, he was not to be seen on the streets of the city. His sole excursions away from the house were to buy food or for an occasional walk in the nearby park. Before long, Nolan had become a forgotten man. There were those who thought he had died. On the occasion that he was seen after dusk in the park, there was perhaps a moment of shock, as though a ghost had been sighted. In this way ten years went by. And then there was that letter.

Nolan returned from the mailbox and once again took his seat in the study. He was thinking of Sophie. It was fourteen years ago. For months Nolan had been preparing for an expedition to excavate an ancient Jewish cemetery just north of Jerusalem in what was still called Palestine by archaeologists. Some weeks before his departure, a woman appeared in his office in answer to an announcement he had placed with several colleges. Sophie was young, about thirty, blond, he saw, but not beautiful. No, very far from beautiful. Large and ruddy, rather, with an air of athletic grace and strength.

"What can you do?" he had asked her.

"I can draw to scale. I can take photographs, keep records. I will do anything." (Nolan saw that she would.) She stirred the air with her fingers as she spoke. He had hoped for a man as his assistant.

"You would have to wear a hat," he said, "for the sun." (Sophie smiled.)

"If there are any discomforts," she said, "you won't hear about them." Then, earnest, imploring: "I want to go with you." When he hesitated, she repeated it. "I want to go." Still Nolan remained silent. "I could carry a footlocker up Mount Everest." She smiled. "I would walk barefoot to Palestine . . ."

. . . for a touch of his nether lip, he finished the quote from *Othello* mentally. "All right, then," he said aloud. "We'll go." And that was that.

As happens often on field trips, Nolan and Sophie had become relaxed, easy, even playful with each other. It was toward the end of their third month in Palestine. The last of the tombs cut into the soft limestone had just been opened. The diggers had uncovered there the skeleton of a young male. About twenty-five years old, Nolan estimated. He had been crucified. A seven-inch nail had been driven through both heel bones so that the feet were fixed side by side. The tip of the nail had been bent and curled upon itself by the hammering and so was left as it had been set and not withdrawn to be used again as was usually done. Both femurs had been broken by blunt blows. All this Nolan deduced and dictated to Sophie. All this she copied in her notebook. In the wall of the cave just above the tomb, Hebrew letters had been cut, "Y-H-W-H-N-N B-N H-G-G-W-L" he spelled aloud and translated:

"*Yehohanan ben Hagakol*. His name." Together they had knelt in the dust, measuring, recording.

"Five feet, eight inches in height," he said.

"Why are the thigh bones broken?"

"To hasten death," he explained. "To permit burial before nightfall. It was the custom among the Jews."

"What had he done?" she wanted to know. "What crime?"

"Political, I suppose. That was the usual."

"Such a fine-boned, slender, graceful body," she said. "It has harmony."

"You'll never make a scientist," he told her. "You're too senti-mental. To us a body is what it is—skin, muscle, bone, nothing more. Scientists are sensible. We have clean, straight minds."

"I don't believe a word of that," she said. (Nolan had to smile in spite of himself.)

"You archaeologists are like that boy in Grimm's fairy tales, the one who couldn't feel horror. He would play with corpses as though they were toys. In the end, he had to be sent away by his father to learn how to shudder. Scientists should be made to do that."

"How did the tale end?"

"I don't remember. And it doesn't matter. You think that the passage of two thousand years distances you from horror, excuses you from feeling it? Not in the least. Horror is what keeps us from behaving with even greater cruelty than we do. Personally, I suspect there is a bit of necrophilia in every archaeologist."

"But anyway," he had told her, "he is not perfect. Look." He held the skull up to show her the cleft in the bony palate, the con-genital absence of the right canine tooth, the way the other teeth were displaced abnormally.

"The face, too, is asymmetrical. It slants a bit from one side to the other. The eye sockets are different heights, as are the aper-tures of the nose. It is called hemiatrophy of the face. What have you gotten so far?"

"Right forehead flattened, jaw asymmetrical," she read from her notebook. "Perhaps . . ." she murmured wistfully, "perhaps he had a beard that would hide it?" He turned then and looked at her as though for the first time. She was smiling softly. Two weeks later Nolan asked her to become his wife. They were married in Jerusalem.

"Yehohanan—Jonathan," she had whispered to him after they had made love for the first time. "If we have a son."

▼   ▼   ▼

It was a September evening not long after they had returned from Palestine. Sophie and Nolan were undressing for bed.

"What's that?" He pointed to a place on her thigh where the muscle was writhing beneath the skin. Sophie, too, stared at the spot, ran her fingers over it briefly, then took them back.

"Do you feel anything?" he had asked her. Sophie shook her head.

"There it goes again," he said and pointed to her other leg. "The gastrocnemius muscle. It is fasciculating—it is evidence of muscle-tissue distress." Then, turning away, "We'll have to find out."

A week later the doctor announced, "Amyotrophic lateral sclerosis, Lou Gehrig's disease. She is unusually young for it." The doctor was speaking to Nolan as though Sophie were not present.

"But what . . . ?" Nolan had asked.

"It just happens," he said.

The next evening, she who was not clumsy dropped a plate.

"I'll get it," he said, going for the dustpan and brush, but she had gotten there first. There was something grotesquely agile, fierce, about the way she hurried to beat him to it. That night Sophie had gone to bed early. She had left the bedside lamp lit for him. Hours later, while undressing, he saw that she was lying awake. She seemed to him suddenly unreachable, already lost.

"What are you thinking?" he asked her.

"I was thinking what a relief it must have been for Adam when Eve was created. Then he could take his mind away from the serious business of tending the Garden of Eden and lose himself in the mysteries of a woman's body." But she had said it too brightly.

"What are you thinking?" he asked again.

"Nothing, then."

"But you are always thinking. Tell me."

"Nothing," she repeated and reached to turn off the light as if to turn off the possibility of thinking. When he got into bed there was exactly that silence as when someone is beating a drum.

The first year and a half had seen a rapid progression of the paralysis. Her legs were sticks that could not hold her up. Three times she had toppled from them to lie in ruins on the floor. Once she had cut her chin. He had gotten a wheelchair. Since then, the decline had been slower, but no less relentless. By the end of the third year only her left arm retained the gross, unrefined movements of shoulder and elbow. In the fingers, nothing. Night after night he lay awake listening to her efforts to rest. But sleep was slow in coming to her. When it came, it was scarcely less harsh in appearance than death. They had become strangely formal with each other, each maintaining a certain reserve. The disease seemed to demand it of them, the way a guest in the house draws forth unwonted politeness between the hosts. Only once had she given herself up to sorrow in his presence, had lain awake the whole night sobbing. By morning her blue eyes had been wept all the way out to gray.

"Sophie," he had said, "you must try."

"Try what?" she said like a child. Then Nolan knew that he would never leave her, that he would stay until whatever came. For between husband and wife lay a secret. The truth was that they no longer loved each other. Perhaps even, he thought, she had never really loved him. But in the beginning, he had loved her—he was sure that he had. It was nobody's fault. The marriage had simply withered after their return from Palestine, as though it had been a plant native to the Holy Land and only able to flourish in that stony soil. But by then the disease had come to live in the house with them, and the secret had to be kept.

With the passage of time, Sophie's speech had lost all intelligibility. First to go were the consonants. Initially, she had tried, and her battle to speak terrified and repelled him. Even her head took part in the effort, tossing to disgorge a trapped word. Her shoulders, too, hunched to fling a syllable. Through the distorted working lips, he would watch the clumsy tongue, too large by far, searching for the palate, the teeth—something with which to make contact—and then watch it wallow back each time into the trough of her mouth. Even the vowels lost their full value and had to settle for less. Thus, *hike* became *haak*; *pool* became *pull*. And all the sounds awash in the saliva that she was unable to clear. Once begun, each gargled vowel could not be braked but had to bubble itself out to extinction in the thick glairy mucus. To Nolan, she seemed a hardworking cistern, full of hollow pipe noises. Again and again, he would clear his own throat, as though by doing so hers would come unclogged. At last, she fell silent. Nolan rented a portable suction machine. When the saliva hung in gluey strands from her lips, he would use it.

"Certain diseases," she had said once, when she could still articulate, "certain diseases make an aristocrat of you."

"What are you talking about?"

"Tuberculosis. Anemia."

"That is silly," he had said. But at the time he did not see what lay ahead. Now, for Nolan, the rattling of her phlegm was the rattling of chains on his legs.

Nolan hired a practical nurse to tend her during the day when he was at his laboratory. In the evening and at night, he nursed her himself. Over a period of time, he had acquired a whole repertoire of bedside utterances, the way one becomes fluent in a foreign language by living abroad.

"No point in presenting an untidy foot to the world," he would say and bathe her feet.

"What's this?" He would feign surprise upon finding her sweating and half-naked, after a night of battle with the bedclothes. But he wasn't made for it. The whole process disgusted him. His dreams were of the desert, sandstorms. Weaker and weaker she grew, more and more exhausted. When he carried her from bed to chair, her body in his arms was a series of hollows. Even the backs of her hands were scooped where the muscles had atrophied. Her palms and soles were smooth and pink from disuse, like an infant's. The first time she lost control of her bowels, she was sitting in the wheelchair. When the smell declared itself, she burst into sudden abrupt laughter, which died out in a choking fit from which he had to suction her back. He had become afraid to feed her, considering the chaos of her swallowing, the way nothing in her mouth—tongue, throat, lips—worked to any kind of coordinated effect. Each spoonful that he turned into her mouth held the possibility of asphyxiation. Each time he raised the spoon to her lips, he thought: Can she?

"A feeding tube," the doctor suggested. "It will not be too uncomfortable. A very fine plastic tube. It is passed through your nostril," he explained to Sophie, "and into your stomach. It will simplify matters." Again Sophie had laughed, as though the word *nostril* were the funniest thing in the world, then choked on it. The nurse wheeled her into the bathroom.

"Will it be a long time?" Nolan asked.

"Yes," said the doctor. "That is the way it goes."

When the nurse wheeled Sophie back into the examining room, Nolan saw that she was shaking her head. She did not speak, of course, only wagged her head, sending a tinsel of saliva swinging.

"She doesn't want the feeding tube," he told the doctor. "She will not have it."

"Well, then," said the doctor. In his voice a skin of concern overlay the granite of disapproval. "The alternative is intravenous feeding."

"All right," said Nolan.

"But can you do it?"

"Yes."

And each morning he hung the bottle on the pole, ran the fluid through the tubing to rinse it of air, and inserted the needle into her vein. After taping the needle in place, Nolan would sit by the bed, and together Sophie and he would watch the slow pendant drops, each one bearing the reflection of this hated room into her bloodstream.

"Would you like me to read to you, Sophie?" When she nodded, submitting, he would open the book to a place, clear his throat, and begin.

"Chapter Two—*Jane Eyre*."

It was the fourteenth of October. He could remember exactly. Nolan had come into the bedroom to change the bottle of fluid. He saw at once that she was engaged in a struggle. She was trying to speak. Her mouth and face, even her neck joined, and her shoulders lifted as though to shrug the words from her lips.

"What is it?" he asked her. "Do you want the bedpan? Are you hungry? Do you need to be suctioned?" On and on she worked, ignoring each of his suggestions.

"Sophie . . ." he said, "what?" But already he had fastened his gaze to her lips, for he knew that the words she was working to release would set him free. Then she who could not speak spoke.

"Kill me," she said, firing the two syllables point-blank into his face. No humid panting air, this, but words that, had they been rocks upon which twin beacons had been placed, would have stood out in a wild sea, such was the clarity with which she uttered them.

That night Nolan dreamed of the crucified Jew that he and Sophie had studied together in Palestine. In the dream, Nolan saw him again with clinical exactitude: the way he had been hung from the cross—the parallel feet transfixed at the heels by the great bent nail; the broken legs adjacent to one another; the knees doubled, the right one overlapping the left; the trunk twisted, and the left buttock resting on a narrow transverse board set there to prolong his agony; the arms, each one stabbed in the forearm by a nail, outstretched. In his dream, the Jew was bearded, just as Sophie had hoped. His narrow chest heaved in the throes of slow asphyxiation. Nolan heard the rattle in the throat of the dying Jew. The end could not be far off. He awoke suddenly and jerked to a sitting position to hear the to-and-fro rattling of her phlegm as she slept. From dream into waking there had been no intermission in the sound. Sophie, too, awakened at his sudden movement. Had he cried out in his sleep?

"It's nothing," he told her. "Go back to sleep."

Nolan rose and went into the bathroom. In the mirror his eyes were red as those of a hunter who has tracked all day, all night. His skin was hot to the touch. He returned to the bedroom and lay down beside his wife. But Nolan did not sleep. For a long time he watched her labor back toward unconsciousness, listened to the strangled sounds that never stopped even in the deepest sleep. When he was sure, he slipped the pillow from beneath his head, knelt on the bed, raised the pillow high in both hands, and lowered it over Sophie's face. Either she never woke up, or she did and yielded. At last the rattling ceased. In the silence he watched her hand for evidence. After a few minutes her fingers had trembled slightly, then lay still.

Nolan never went to his office or laboratory again. The next day he sent a letter of resignation to the president of the university, insisting that no inquiry be made on the matter of his resignation. It was not open to discussion. The decision was private, irrevocable.

▼　　▼　　▼

Two weeks after receiving Foulkes's letter, Nolan was on his way to England. Outwardly the trip was made by plane, train, and automobile. But right from the start Nolan had the sense of being transported by other means entirely. With each passing hour, he was plunging deeper into himself. En route, he gazed out the windows of the conveyances, watching lands go bright and dark, bright and dark, and wondered at how far over the past ten years he had retreated into solitude. He had long ago lost all enthusiasm for field expeditions, for archaeology itself. Would he be able to do it? For it had been his intention, from that first moment, to study the bog, its origin, composition, all the flora and fauna of it. There must be no respectful distance between him and it. But first he would go to the museum, to the Lindow Man.

Soon Nolan was standing before the glass case in which Lindow Man had been placed. The detached leg had been put in what would have been its normal position. The case had been mounted on a pedestal so that the display could be viewed at eye level. The printed legend on the wall made it clear that the temperature and humidity inside the case were carefully controlled and that the man had been treated with tannic acid and other preservatives, then soaked in Turkish red oil. Collodion had been injected beneath the skin here and there to prevent shrinkage.

"You can expect twelve percent shrinkage even after that." It was the curator explaining. He led Nolan to another room, where they could examine the color-coded X-rays, thermographic images, holography—all of the diagnostic tests to which the specimen had been subjected.

"He was young," said Nolan.

"About twenty-five, from the bone development."

"What was in the stomach?"

"A sort of gruel of barley, linseed, and another seed they call 'gold of pleasure' around these bogs. And knotweed. That was his last meal."

"Then it must have been early spring, this time of year," said Nolan. "From the seeds."

"Yes, a sacrifice to bring on an early growing season." The curator laughed brightly.

Later, Nolan returned alone to where Lindow Man lay in the glass case. He was a man in the very prime of life, with long arms and a body rigged all over with muscles and sinews. There was something fetal about the face, as though he were not really dead but in a state of becoming, a creature in a chrysalis and with the intent of emerging. Bones all swaddled in skin, and pillowed in peat. The feet were highly arched; the pleated skin was resin-colored and fused with the muscles to form a single mass that had the grain of several kinds of wood. The beard was reddish, perhaps a week's growth. The hair, too, reddish and short. The cap of it sat close upon his head. And tight about his neck, the torque of braided rawhide with which he had been strangled. Otherwise he was naked. A twig had been inserted beneath the noose. It had been used for twisting, to tighten the cord. A single loop of intestine, like the handle of a jar, protruded from a rent in the abdomen. The head was bowed, the face turned toward the right armpit. It was self-absorbed, without the least expression of pain. What, then? Resignation? It was as though at the last moment he had experienced something that had caused whatever contorted features to relent into somber tranquillity. Still, like all martyrs, he was enameled with suffering, all in brown monotone, incorruptible. All at once, Nolan was overcome by a wave of dizziness and nausea. The floor might have tilted. He lurched to regain his balance. Just as quickly, the feeling passed. The next morning, Nolan left for Lindow Moss.

▼   ▼   ▼

It was the afternoon of the first of April when the taxi drove away, leaving him at the door of a house that was more a cottage than an inn. Few of the amenities, Foulkes had warned: a pub with rooms upstairs and within walking distance of Lindow Moss. The inn itself was one of two dozen crooked, tilting cottages, each wearing a dense mane of thatch, that comprised the village of Mobberley. The only difference was that while the others were hunchbacked, only this one was swayed like an old horse. No two walls of the building were at right angles to each other. This, Nolan understood, was from the slow drifting of the peat in the bog that pressed in upon the cottage.

His room at the top of the stairs was furnished with a narrow bed, a chair, a writing table, and a heavy wooden footlocker such as is used by sailors. A fireplace occupied one corner. On a washstand there was a china pitcher and washbowl, white with a faded pale-green design of leaves. In the footlocker, a few scientific tracts on the botany and fauna of the countryside, which Nolan had requested from Foulkes. From his own library he had brought a text on the archaeology of Danish and German fens. Looking down at the passing road from the single window, Nolan felt an unaccountable surge of happiness. It seemed to him, though he knew it untrue, that his coming to this place was in fact a returning.

Without unpacking, Nolan left the inn. A narrow road descended in the direction of the bog. It was less a road, actually, than a sunken rutted lane, here and there vaulted by the slender branches of trees. A hundred paces down this path, and already he could no longer see the cottages of the village nor any of the sheep that had free run of the fields, nor any sign of life. The path bore him along at its own slow cadence until, passing through a bank of low shrubs and trees, it seemed to plunge beneath the bog itself. Unlike at home, where greenery had been abundant, here spring was installing itself by the smallest advances—an occasional willow brightening, the red knobs of birch buds—as though in all the world only this bog were exempt from the agitation of the season. Soon the lane narrowed to a single-file footpath, then petered out altogether.

Stepping through a small copse of alder bushes, Nolan found himself at last before a vast, flat silver expanse. What a great stopped clock it was. The overwhelming impression was of soddenness, with here and there pools of iron-colored water, each with its pelt of bulrushes, and in between, hummocks of sphagnum moss. No path traversed the bog; it suffered no trampling. Nolan stooped and dug his hand like a spade into the soft muck, letting it seep through his fingers. It seemed to him primitive, undifferentiated tissue, full of potential. If he had been expecting a sinister place, an ulcerous crater in the land, he was instead confronted with what seemed for all the world like a life-giving womb. To study this bog, to know it down to the least plant and stone—he would rinse his mind of all else. Already, bits of evidence were presenting themselves to him: the scent of thyme freshly crushed by a tiny paw, the distant low drum of thunder. All at once, standing at the edge of the bog, Nolan shuddered. Was it from the cold? It was as though he had returned to an empty theater after the performance was over. In another moment the eeriness had passed.

That evening he took his meal at the pub that occupied the ground floor of the cottage. In fact, it was a large kitchen with a dozen or so oak tables and chairs, a bar, and a large stove. The landlord inquired:

"What brings you to Mobberley?"

"Lindow Moss."

"About the man, is it?"

Nolan nodded.

"A scientist, then?"

"Yes, I am."

"They found one once," said the landlord. "It was just his skin with nothing inside. No bones. A whole bag of skin and a pair of shoes. Might've been a snake but for the shoes."

That first night, Nolan could not sleep for excitement; his mind was full of Lindow Moss, its curdling, enhaloed mist. How had the bog been formed? He had to know. What layers did it comprise? What was the natural history of this place? If he had to drain it to the bottom, he would learn its secrets. It seemed to him ironic that the end of all this wetness was fire—the bog turning slowly to peat, whose destiny it was to fill a hearth with heat and light.

▼   ▼   ▼

On the morning of April 2, Nolan rose before dawn, bathed, and breakfasted, and then went down the narrow sunken road to the edge of the bog. For the first week he did not enter the bog but remained at the periphery, pacing out and mapping the circumference, now and then pausing to write in his notebook or draw the lines of a map. The cottage lay on the southern edge of the bog. Along the northern margin Nolan came upon a group of men harvesting peat. Bent double, with their triangular shovels lifting and falling, they followed like gleaners in the wake of the HY-MAC. Nolan decided to concentrate his study in the portion of the fen nearest the cottage. There he could work without the distraction of unwanted company. Even so, there would be mornings so clear and quiet that he could hear the men calling out to one another, and the grinding of gears when the HY-MAC was shifted into reverse.

On April 13, Nolan wrote in his notebook:

The area of the fen is 12 x 7^1/$_2$ miles at greatest diameter, and is vaguely rhomboid in shape. The fen itself is a flatland devoid of trees and hedges except all around the outer rim. It was formed thousands of years ago by the overflow from a catchment basin in the surrounding uplands, where seawater from the inrushing tide was trapped. This salt-calcereous water was sweetened in its course by the many small rivers that wind through this country—Witham, Welland, Nene, Great and Little Ouse, Lark, and Nar—names as sweet as their waters. From this mixture of fresh and salt water there was deposited the sand and silt that was to become the floor of the bog.

Long since cut off from the surface flow of these rivers, the water ceased to flow. It became stagnant and deficient in oxygen. Saturated with soil acids and rich in tannin, the water is brown in color, shot through with iron gray. The whole bog has the odor of cave walls and mushrooms.

Over time, the bog pools became laced with submerged leafy aquatic plants. Generations of mosses, ferns, and sedges lived and died here. These millennia of organic matter were slowly packed together and compressed into peat. All around the edges of the pools there are molybdenum-consuming alder bushes and small trees—mostly aspen, birch, and pine. It has not always been a place of low vegetation and slim trees. Once, great forests governed here, all now sunk beneath the muck. Now and then I see the stripped crown of a toppled bog oak rising above the surface. One of these measures ninety feet in length and is entirely lacking in side branches, which were lost in the ancient competition for light in the once dense forest. The trunk of the tree is surprisingly undecayed in these anaerobic conditions.

Day followed day, and on each of them Nolan patrolled the bog, dispatched his mind like a sentry to pace through the mist, listing the insects, birds, and animals that he saw, collecting specimens of the plant life, observing the changes brought about by each succeeding hour. Sometimes he felt that he was seeing the plants and animals for the first time, that they had never been seen before. Sometimes, in the confusion of the mist, which gave to everything a kind of hazy transparency, he felt that he was seeing them even before they had been created. On May 4, Nolan listed these plants:

Nymphea alba—the white water lily; *nuphar luteum*—the yellow water lily. At dusk these water lilies, the shiest of flowers, are drawn beneath the surface for the night. Then, only their flat green pads lie on the surface. Is it the retraction of the stem that pulls the flower under, only to elongate and thrust it up at dawn? Also seen: cattails, sphagnum, heather, cotton grass, andromeda, heath, cranberry, bog asphodel. And these moisture-tolerant bushes: sallow, guelder rose, buckthorn.

Girdling each bog pool grow giant sword sedges whose leaves are razor sharp. And every sword drawn! I believe them capable of cutting to the bone. These sword sedges bend into a mat that can be walked upon. The big leaf blades of the bulrushes of which the roof of the cottage is made blow like flags in the wind.

With his daily tabulations finished, Nolan would set his back against a buckthorn tree in the companionship of his drawn-up and hugged knees, smoking the cigarettes of patience and contentment and listening to the piping of birds, the thumping of frogs, the hissing of leaves, all of the sounds by which the bog was making itself known to him. Later, lying in bed, he would feel the influence of the bog right up to the moment of sleep—and thereafter, for the bog had begun to pervade his dreams as well.

The entry for May 28 read:

Each day there is no following in yesterday's footprints. You take a step and moments later the impression has been smoothed out, as though no one had walked there. Penetration of the bog on foot is safe only during the daytime, when progress can be made by jumping from one island of moss to another. Even then, the footing is uncertain and you are apt to find yourself ankle-deep in the muck. Of two pools sounded, one is twelve, the other ten feet in depth. Once, perhaps, small boats were pulled here. Just beneath the surface float the long tendrils of waterweeds, closely tangled. At a depth of four feet the pool is no longer water but a mixture of sand, silt, and organic matter. The sounding poles, when let go, disappear slowly beneath the surface, grasped by quicksand. It is an eerie thing to feel the stick taken from your hand as though there were a voracious intelligence at the bottom of the bog, something that must be fed.

June 3:
Colze, whose seeds were once crushed and used for lamp oil.
Cannabis—used as it is today in the inhalation of burning hemp seed.
Poppies, for opium.

Woad or "glastrum"—a blue-dye plant with which the ancient British warriors painted their faces to frighten the Roman legionnaires.

Eels, frogs, fish, many birds. Today: a species of speckled yellowlegs, several kinds of heron, a rail, the usual wrens and sparrows.

Clover, spelt rye, Yorkshire fog, rye grass, goosefoot, buttercup, lady's-mantle, black nightshade, yarrow, wild chamomile, smooth hawk's-beard.

By the first of May, the hard, sour winter had gone soft and sweet like a rotting apple. New birds had appeared—peewit, lark, curlew, and ravens that stabbed for worms in the peat. The color of the pools had deepened from iron gray to umber. Here and there yellow and white water lilies broke the dark water. Some days the mist thickened so that only when it parted was he permitted a few yards of visibility.

At dusk he would leave the bog and walk up the narrow path to the inn. His room suited him as no other ever had. The lack of adornment, the meagerness of its furnishings, suggested less a chamber than an antechamber, a place of transience in which any sign of opulence would have been inappropriate. In such a room, one has not arrived; one is en route. Yet once inside, with the door closed and the flames of a turf fire tottering in the grate, Nolan found a pleasure and refuge he had not known in years. In the evening, he would spread his maps on the table and shade in the details of the bog he had noted during the day. Then, laying out the plant specimens he had gathered, he matched them with the descriptions in the botany manual, taking a poet's relish in the names of each—asphodel, cinquefoil, pimpernel, sweet gale, bog orchid, violet.

Once he remained at the bog all through the night. Now and then, while listening to the leathery flap of wings and the stridulation of the insects, he felt upon his cheek the cool fingers of mist. In the utter darkness he knew the clairvoyance of the blind. When at last he heard the singing of the birds who had preceded him into the dawn, it was as though he were listening into the future. At his feet the bog yawned and awoke, as the darkness began to melt and dilute itself. That morning, he came upon a ball of green adders lying entwined and slowly writhing on the path, and a small crow-ripped splotch of blood and fur.

▼　　▼　　▼

On the fifteenth day of July Nolan had a recurrence of the illness he had experienced while at the museum. He was standing at dusk in a small grove of slender trees when he had an abrupt sense of dislocation, as though he were standing on the bank of a river and it was the earth that was moving while the stream itself stood still. Had he not leaned against a tree trunk, he might have fallen. All at once a terrified birch began talking to him, whispering some frantic secret or other. Nolan tried to steady the tree with his hand but it would not stop trembling. He pressed his ear against the white bark to listen but could not understand. There he remained until the delirium subsided, leaving him exhausted. Night had descended by the time he slowly made his way homeward.

From then on, each day and several times a day, the dizziness and fever returned with a kind of undulating rhythm, each time leaving him in a state of depletion. The plants and animals that had before appeared to him in all their clarity were blurred, ambiguous. His dedication to the orderly study of the bog ebbed. No longer did he search for specimens. The entries in his notebook became shorter, more fragmentary—sometimes a single phrase. The entry for July 28 was simply the word "pimpernel." Whole days went by when he wrote nothing at all. Maps and data, he thought, tell of no past. Once he spent an entire morning watching a dark-purple insect, a beetle perhaps, polishing itself. Now when he opened the notebook that lay on the oak table in his room Nolan did not recognize the handwriting in it as his own. Nor could he read what was written there, as though it were in a foreign language.

He who had gone beardless all his life forgot to shave himself for days. His appetite dwindled, and meals were random. He grew thin and pale. Still, out of long habit, he continued each morning to wash himself with cold water that he poured from the pitcher on the washstand. The shock of the cold water on his face and chest returned him from a night of phantoms. And, somehow, it seemed a minor ritual that each day entitled him to present himself at the bog.

By September it had become an effort to rise from sitting, to walk. He would aim his foot at a hummock of moss, only to misjudge and find himself ankle-deep in water. It was as though he had lost the exact sense of where he stood in relation to the world. Nolan now felt himself no longer a scientist on an expedition but an aspirant waiting in the bog. For what? He did not know. All his old contempt for science returned. Archaeologists, he thought, anatomists—they scrape things down to what they think to be their essence. In the end, they, too, are destined to live in the merest conjecture. The most anyone can have is an inkling. His own life work, all that raising of the doors of tombs—for what? Better, he thought, to simply bind together the hands of the dead, and avert one's gaze. No. Lindow Moss could not be measured, cataloged. It was not the surface that would reveal to him his destiny but the deep mass of the bog itself. If he had learned anything in these months, it was that things are not what they are but what they become upon immersion.

Often now Nolan would stay on into the twilight. He was like a sailor who, even on land, must keep the sea within his sights. In the dusk, silence flew past in the shape of an owl. There was the softness of moths. From time to time, the greenish lichen and the yellow of the gorse would become an unhealthy phosphorescence that jumped from place to place. Any moment then the whole bog could become a Sabbath moor where nightly revels took place.

Once he had fallen asleep and was awakened in the darkness of night by something nibbling at his fingers and with a pain beneath his fifth rib as though a shovel were being thrust into his flesh. He pulled himself erect, then walked toward the path, holding out his arms like a somnambulist. It was not fear that gripped him, but the sense of having been muffled in blindness and deafness.

Narrower and narrower grew the path from the cottage, like an isthmus through which he must squeeze to reach the flat, vacant stretch of the bog. The room in which he had once taken refuge and comfort seemed now hardly more than a closet where the air was stale and heavy, as deficient in oxygen as the bog itself. He tried to think what it might be that suffocated him here—the insomniac bed? the chair? the oaken table? Perhaps it was the ticking of a clock or the raveled edge of a curtain. Sometimes in the throes of a sleepless night, his body throbbing with fever, he would think: I must leave this place. There is still time. But as quickly as the thought came, it would vanish. How would he leave? His coming had taken place in a dream; his departure must be by the same route. A dream cannot be willed. Nor, in fact, did he want to leave. His task was only to wait and, when the time came, to submit.

In that part of the bog he had chosen for his vigil, he was alone. Hunched in his greatcoat, hands in his pockets, Nolan stood hour after hour, motionless as one of the bushes, watching the elastic mist stiffen and relax. At such times, his thoughts would drift to the Lindow Man himself—the massive block of bone and muscle that had become his only companion. Try as he might to find in the terrain of the bog, in its flora and fauna, a point of consolidation for his life, he could not, and in the end he had drifted farther and farther from reality. By the beginning of October, the waiting in this no-man's land had become his sole function, the reason for his existence.

▼　　　▼　　　▼

It was the twenty-sixth of October. Everything with wings to fly had flown south for the winter, except the crows. All day it had threatened to rain. The anticipation had worn down his spirit, hollowed him out. To the wind, he was no different from cloud or branch. Was it fatigue or dizziness or the incessant siffling of the grasses that filled his head with confusion? His thoughts were fragmented, random. Before he was aware of it, night had fallen. In the gathered dusk he could make out the birches, their bleached arms upraised in grief; later they were only a grove of bones that disappeared into the darkness. Nolan shivered in the cold. The prospect of rising to his feet, gathering his gear, and finding his way back to the cottage seemed physically daunting. He would light a fire, make coffee. After that, he would go. Rising, he went in search of kindling. It was no easy thing to find wood that was dry enough. From a birch tree he peeled small scrolls of bark; from a pine, he broke twigs; there was a single patch of dead sphagnum. With these, he began. The first three matches failed. He had only two more. Nolan joined the everlasting battle between fire and water with all his concentration, throwing his breath and his will on the side of a flame, fending off the twin forces of damp and dark until at last there was flame. He added to the kindling, fetched a small log, then a larger one. Squatting by what he had made, he poured coffee from a pouch at his belt, water from a bottle into a pan, and waited for it to boil. The fire gave off a dense, bittersweet smoke. Nolan lit a cigarette and sipped the coffee. In the orange glow he imagined a tribe of wild Britons—their campfires, their herds and granaries, their stone houses. He saw their blue-painted faces as they readied themselves for battle. In his reverie he held in his hands their clay bowls, their picks made of deer horn. He crouched with their sentries around a fire over which an iron pot hissed, listened as one of the men began a singsong chant while the others nodded in recognition, then yawned and sank deeper into their furs. His thoughts went to the ancient sacrifice and its victim. Had they given him the blessing of wine made from wild cranberries, barley, and fermented honey? Had he been prepared with the smoke of cannabis or with the juice of poppies? Had he been blindfolded? With the flames of the fire rising and falling like voices in a choir, Nolan gazed into the darkness and saw the man, naked save for the plaited noose about his neck, his cropped hair, a stubble of beard; saw him led by priests to the edge of a pool; saw the tightening of the stick, the man's face darkening, his bulging eyes, the look of . . . was it resignation? . . . on his face at the last, the body growing limp, falling. Had he at one time tried to flee? Had he then to be captured and restrained? Or had he accepted? There are always those who offer themselves.

He thought of Lindow Man, of his tiny unremarked, patient death, of how he had lain like a seed in a slumber of peat for two thousand years, in a kind of secret permanence while all else— water, earth, birds, animals, human beings—was changing. How he only, of all his kind, had lasted until he had been harvested and lifted up into the light of day, beautifully remote, bandaged in his own skin, and been placed in a tabernacle, inviting worship. What was it they called him? Pete Marsh. Sophie was right: It is the vast expanse of time that gives them the boldness. And Nolan remembered how he had knelt on the bed beside her, the pillow held aloft, how he had glanced back over his shoulder to see if anyone, any*thing* were witnessing.

When the fire had died out, Nolan doused the few embers and felt his way back to the path. It was midnight before he lay down to sleep.

In this way Nolan lived out the enchantment of autumn, watching the phantoms of fog floating close and far, listening to the singing of the insects, the hiss of the bulrushes, until slowly, imperceptibly, an inkling gathered in his mind—an inkling of what it was that he had come to Lindow Moss to seek; his own freely chosen death. Only the time was in doubt. Resting in a bed of rushes, he had the invisibility of a hidden animal, the silence, the knowledge that only he was there. He had at last set himself apart from all his kind in order to prepare himself.

▼   ▼   ▼

When Nolan returned to the spavined cottage with its mane of thatch in the evening, he would take his supper alone and in silence, then linger in the pub sipping the strong bitter local ale. Shortly after dark, the place began to fill with people. It was a men's pub, entirely without pretension. No effort had been made to decorate the dark wood paneling. Nothing hung from the ceiling beams. The lighting, pewter sconces set at intervals along the walls, was dim. Each time the door opened, a slab of thick damp air was sliced off into the room, and floating in with it a new face that hung uncertainly for a moment, then swam through the layered smoke to settle along a wall or lower itself to a table. The low rumble of voices was punctuated by the sound of darts thudding into cork. Now and then a man laughed, another coughed. Night after night Nolan sat in a land of impenetrable strangeness from which he was set apart by a wall of words, noises, silences. Even the tables and chairs seemed to join in his alienation. There were never more than twenty men in the pub at any given time, and those for the most part the same ones each night. He knew them only by sight, and from the briefest of greetings. They had bony, triangular faces like the shovels they used to dig for peat, and sunken places at the temples and cheeks to match their hollow voices, long-cut straight dark hair. Even indoors, several of them wore their old-fashioned yellow oilskin raincoats.

It was the middle of November. The nights were cold. Nolan, out of fatigue or inertia, had remained in the pub later than usual. Seated at his table in a corner, he had a premonition that the door was about to open. He braced himself for the inrush of cold air, and turned to see a woman carrying a guitar case slip quickly through the door and make her way to a table at the inmost part of the room. Along the way she was greeted by some of the men, who smiled and spoke to her in a dialect that Nolan could not understand, and raised their glasses to her. It was apparent that they knew her. She was, Nolan saw, no longer young—about forty, and with long damp hair whose mass hung heavy in a snood. She carried her head very high, as though it were pulled backward by the weight of that hair. Once she had taken her seat, the innkeeper brought a glass of beer to her table. The woman lit a cigarette and sat calm and smiling and alone. At precisely nine o'clock she rose, took the guitar from its case, and went to sit on a high stool in the center of the room. At once, the pub hauled itself in, grew quieter. Now the woman struck the guitar with the flat of her hand. She began to sing—a ballad of the region, Nolan supposed, since now and then the men would join in a refrain. The words had no meaning for him. From the first, Nolan could not take his gaze from her bare white arms, which again and again departed from her body to cradle the guitar, then, giving one last leap at the end of a song, settled to her sides. Her voice was tired, ripe, an overflow from her throat, full of viscid diphthongs that she let drip from the end of her tongue. To Nolan, she seemed to emit a gospel of sensuality that he heard as much with his skin as with his ears. Her mouth opened, and he could see her nimble tongue, a wild fluttering as of a moth at the back of her throat.

He had not looked with much interest or a more than momentary curiosity at any woman in the ten years since Sophie's death. It was as though the taking of Sophie's life had exacted that portion of his own in which the desire for human contact had been housed. But now each evening Nolan waited for the door of the pub to swing open, for the woman to appear. Once, while she was singing, she had looked up from the guitar to meet his solemn gaze. She had smiled then and nodded her head. In greeting? No, he thought, not in greeting. What, then? And then there came the night when, after she had finished singing, the woman came to the table in the corner where he sat.

"You," she said, with accusation. "They say you go to the Lindow Moss all day and half the night." She lit a cigarette and laughed the smoke out of her lungs.

"What do you want there? That smelly place. Nothing but peat. Is it the peat you are wanting? And there is quicksand. No good will come of it. Once a woman wandered in and was caught in it. They never found her. Never." Softly her voice mocked him.

"What is your name?" he asked.

"Ora," she said. His temples were pounding. Either he would touch her or he would not. For a long moment he looked down at his hand where it rested in his lap, consulting the pattern of veins on the back of it. He watched it lumber up from his thigh like some big graceless bird attempting to fly, saw it flap across the table and come to rest upon hers. And there on that coolness it stayed. She did not draw away. At last, smiling, she took up her guitar and stood.

"I will sing now," she said. Nolan's gaze was lashed to the rim of the glass from which she had drunk, where the outline of her lips in the beer foam remained. He had all he could do to keep from seizing that glass and licking the mark of her mouth from it. To save himself, he spoke again.

"What is it you will sing?"

"It is a song of the River Ouse that runs through this country. A young man is fishing in the Ouse one day. He lets go of his line in order to give his girl a kiss. It is just the same moment that a big trout bites. He is torn between his two desires. In the end he loses both the girl and the fish." When she lifted the guitar to her lap to play, Nolan rose and walked to the foot of the stairs. The wooden staircase creaked under his weight. Dithering with fever, he clung to the railing like a man in a flood, pulling himself up hand over hand. Or was it the whole hollow inn itself that shook and came to rest at the edge of Lindow Moss? His brain flashing with lights, Nolan shouldered into the room at the top of the stairs, collided with the table, and threw himself upon the cot before he would have fallen. A turf fire had been lit in the grate. The faint sounds of the guitar came to him where he lay staring into the darkness. From below came the good-natured smell of beer. Slowly the dizziness passed. Perhaps he slept. When, later, the door opened and he saw her outlined by the frame of it, Nolan was startled.

"Are you all right?" she asked, and stepped to the bed, "What is it?" she whispered. But Nolan did not answer. His silence was less that of one lost in thought—he had no thoughts—than something close to mere animal speechlessness. She reached out and placed her palm on his forehead. Nolan sat up on the edge of the bed.

"You've come," he said.

"Yes," she said simply. Meekly he allowed her to undress him, then watched her clothing fall piece by piece to the floor. Her hands reached over her head, grasping the blouse at opposite shoulders to pull it over her bowed head. When she released her hair from the snood, her throat and arms were upraised like a trumpet. Then she was naked, save for a small gold crucifix at her throat. For Nolan it made her more than naked, translucent.

"What?" she said, looking down at him, for he neither moved nor spoke. "What is it?" And a coil of her hair, heavy as dough, fell across his shoulders. All at once Nolan reached out and seized the standing woman at her hips and drew her between his knees, seized her as though she were a jar he would lift to his mouth to drink. Ora pressed him back upon the bed and with a quick movement lay on top of him, securing him lest he drift away. Nolan felt his flesh stirring beneath the generous hands of the woman, her vehement tongue, and he yielded to the onrush of lust that had lain dormant for ten years and that, like Sophie's paralyzed body, had undergone the atrophy of disuse. He was wild with it. Had it been a thirst, he would have drunk his own blood to slake it. And all the while he spied on her face, searching there for clues. Now and then she opened her eyes and gave him a smile, which he took inside himself the way she had taken him inside her body. Above, the gold crucifix flashed, now against his mouth, now his forehead. When the climax approached, he had a moment of fear that he would not survive it.

Almost at once, she offered love again. From the window a bluish moonlight struggled against the orange flames of the fire in the grate. In this dual light he rode her, clinging to the masses of her hair as if to the mane of a horse. To each of his rapturous strokes she responded with a deep sigh, and with each deep sigh she was putting back together his dismembered life. Just once or twice she spoke and then only a word or two, in Gaelic, he thought, uttered out of the oblivion of her body. And all the while, he was concentrating, discovering a long-forgotten secret, immensely curious, and listening for the far-off, tiny coiled thing that was gathering, straining to hear what it might call out to him. At first a whisper rising in a spiral, until at last that booming command: Come!

Nolan awoke to a polished morning. His head was clear, the dizziness gone. Gone, too, the woman. Only . . . the room was filled with the briny smell of the bog, as though it had followed him here and the bed were an island in it. From the window he saw, or thought he saw, Ora hurrying along the road. About her head she was wearing a veil of mist, so he could not be sure. For a moment he had the urge to call out to her, to race down the stairs and retrieve her. But he did not. Later, he asked the innkeeper who she was and where she had gone. A traveling singer, he was told, who had gone on to the next town. Would she be coming back? The landlord shrugged. And all at once Nolan knew that whatever was to happen would happen this day.

▼   ▼   ▼

Nolan made his way down the narrow path to the edge of the bog, where night had fallen. No light so pale as from November's moon. Three times he glanced over his shoulder: There was no one.

Nolan removed his clothing, which he folded neatly and placed in a small pile at the edge of the bog. He glanced down at his pale body. The sight of it saddened him.

Nolan entered the bog. Where he stepped, the turf sank, and water shot up between his toes. Moss sprang from beneath his feet; bulrushes whipped his thighs. Farther and farther Nolan walked, deeper and deeper, leaping like a cat from hummock to hummock. The bog was pliant as flesh.

Toward what? Never mind—he would proceed, giving the bog its head, letting it conduct him to whatever place. On and on, decoding by moonlight the patterns of lichen on rocks, catching the scent of wiry grass where it had been raked by the wind, the semaphore of fireflies. There! This way! A finger of mist pointed to a large sunken pool of iron-colored water that stretched beyond his vision. All at once Nolan detected a movement in the water, small at first, then again. Almost a ripple, perhaps not. Then once more his bare feet caught it—a slow, rhythmic pulse from somewhere far below. Here, he thought. This is the place. And into the smoking caldron Nolan waded until he was knee-deep and there was no longer any scent of the bituminous earth. Below the surface, his feet were pillowed in soft silt that stirred like a cadaver beginning to feel again. All about him rose the bog mutterings—the click of leaf upon leaf, the tiny bursting of a bubble of decay, the arid clamor of insects, a quiet splash, a brief throaty purr. Now he had only to wait.

Nolan peered into the curdling mist and imagined once again what he had so many times before, only now with startling clarity. There was the procession of chanting white-robed priests, each carrying a sprig of mistletoe. There, the three executioners, naked save for short jackets that covered only their chests. And just behind them, the chosen one, led unresisting to this very place where Nolan stood. The man's face was blank, as though all expression had preceded him into death. Only his eyes burned feverishly bright. The loop of rawhide was lowered over his head. At a given sign, a stick was inserted between the noose and his neck. The chanting rose. One of the priests stepped forward and began to twist the stick round and round, tightening the rawhide. The eyes of the man bulged; his face darkened; his tongue protruded. At precisely the moment of asphyxiation, an executioner plunged a knife into the man's abdomen, then ripped upward through the tissues. Blood billowed forth. The stick was twisted further and held. The three priests caught the limp body, lifted it, and cast it facedown into the bog, where it slowly sank from view. All this Nolan saw in the shifting strands of mist.

Imperceptibly at first, but soon undeniably, Nolan felt himself sinking. Already the silt bottom had risen up to swallow his knees and thighs. Minutes later he felt with a kind of voluptuous languor the soft open-textured omnivorous mouth of the bog take in his genitalia and buttocks. It was the last tomb he would open, only this time not to despoil but to enter, himself, and lie down. The water lapped at his navel, and Nolan grew contented, the way a boisterous child curls into its mother's lap and is content to be still. Down and farther down he sank; the stubble of his beard caught at a skirt of mist, snagged, then blew it off in graceful streams. The water covered his nipples. And even as he descended, something else from far below was rising to greet him to lead him down. The bog tightened upon his body. Gripped snugly at the armpits, free at last of gravity, Nolan leaned toward whatever would or would not support him. The pulse in his ear took on a slow, strong regular beat as though his blood and the blood of whatever was submerged were driven by a single heart.

The fever returned. Moment by moment it mounted, and with it came the dizziness. His face ran with sweat. Nolan bowed his head toward the surface of the pool as toward a membrane through which he must pass. Dimly, in deepest shadow, as from the bottom of a well, he saw gazing upwards a face that was gaunt with longing, and behind it, a spray of stars. Suspended at the juncture, he waited for permeability, for the transfusion of swamp that the pores of his skin were opened to receive. Breast to breast, brow to brow, he waited for the moment of crossing over. Nolan took a deep breath, his last, and exhaled. Face, stars, and all were extinguished. There was only a pale smudge on the wavering water. Then he heard a low, long-trapped posthumous groan escape from the fractured pool to lose itself in the curdling mist.

Time passed. About him the bog trembled like the guitar in the woman's arms. Braced and cradled in the heavy mud, Nolan slumped forward, exhausted. When consciousness returned it was as though he had awakened from a deep, enchanted sleep that was more than sleep but less, still much less, than death. And he felt the heavy bog pressing against his body, felt his flesh hardening, cooling. It was difficult to breathe. He drew himself up to ease his chest and discovered rock beneath his feet. The descent had stopped. He explored with his toes, shifting. The hard surface below struck him like a repercussion delivered against the soles of his feet, a recoil transmitted up the length of his body. The glutted bog to which he had aspired with all his heart had thrown him back. All at once, a panic seemed to seize the fog and drive it wisp by wisp from the pool into the trees at the periphery, and now Nolan was afraid. The fear that had awaited him through his months of waiting had found its way into his mind. He felt the water of the pond flowing in his veins. When it reached his heart, he would become a creature of the bog. But suddenly all his dark wish for death had died, and a new, fiercer desire had risen. Nolan wanted to live. He felt bitten all over with longing. Too late, he thought. Too late. He had spent his strength. He cried out for help. Again and again he called into the still, dark bog. Perhaps there would be a shepherd? Or a man digging for peat? There was no one, only the harsh grating of his own voice tapering to a whine, and a low sucking noise that rose from the mud.

He tried to move his legs but could not. The more he struggled, the tighter the grip upon them. It could be hours, days, before he was found. Too late.

The pressure on his chest increased. Nolan remembered how once as a child he had been gravely ill with pneumonia. There had been concern that he might die. He recalled the sense of suffocation, his crying out of the darkness of his bedroom: "I'm choking!" He looked about for something, anything, to grasp and so to pull himself loose. There was nothing, only the shimmering path of moonlight on the smooth surface of the pool. In his despair, he beat at the water with his arms, flailing in wide arcs as if they were oars with which he might row himself to freedom. Nothing. Only there, just there, a point of gleaming at more than arm's reach, a persistent spike of reflected moonlight that outlasted for an instant the roiling of the waters. It was toward this gleam, real or insubstantial, perhaps a brightness only, that Nolan stretched his arm, straining, using his tongue, lips, and teeth, even his gasps, to lengthen his reach, until at last his hand closed upon a hard smooth object. What? An altar horn? Bone? A finger pointing up from the depths upon which for that instant a brightness had settled?

It was a prong of petrified root. With all his might Nolan pulled, grunting like a frog in the mud, which sent up bubbles of decay about him. But still his legs did not move. He rested, counting the seconds, fighting to be calm. Then once again he pulled, shuddering with the force of it, and now the great bog shuddered too, and was torn open by spasms of light. As in a dream, Nolan heard the squelch of suction breaking, felt himself uplifted from the muck and drawn through water, felt upon his thighs filmy tendrils of underwater weeds that would, if they could, wrap about his legs to pull him down. But they gave way. At last he embraced the mass of curved and polished spikes, and he heaved as if to impale himself upon them. There the spent and sobbing man lay. At last his breathing quieted and his clenched fingers relented, but still they did not let go. Lying among the polished roots as though upthrust upon the antlers of a stag, he felt a moment of euphoria, the rapture of a child lifted and held aloft.

With his feet, Nolan could feel extending from the root the trunk of a great fallen oak tree. Long since stripped of its bark, it had the consistency of stone, and slanted upward to end in a crown rising from the pool some sixty feet away. It was this tree without shade or fruit, slippery with mold and algae, that Nolan must mount, whose length he must crawl to safety. He lifted one leg across and thrust himself forward; thrust again, and was astride, gripping the log with his thighs. At last he willed himself to let go of the root and turned to lie upon the barely sunken tree, only his face above the water, gripping the slimy surface with his arms and thighs. With every breath he slid slowly back down toward where the tentacular weeds were waiting and, below them, quicksand. A shiver seized his body. He skidded sideways and his legs slid into the water. He nailed his fingers into the tree and lifted first one leg, then the other, to wrap himself again about the log. Then he forced himself up until his purchase was restored. No man can do it, he thought. No creature with joints. Only a water snake. And he willed himself to move like a thing without bones. Narrowing and drawing himself out like a serpent, he lay his pale pulsing throat along the log. Round and round the tree the serpent locked its many coils. Its eyes glittered with a reptile's patience and instinct. And there he waited until whatever seam there had been between belly and tree had fused, and snake and tree were a single creature of primitive purpose. All this while he saw only what the water snake sees: the slow burst of a bubble, the outsized faceted eye of a water bug scuttling by, a pendant drop of brine, a pale scum of fish spawn. And when he knew that the time had come, he squeezed his muscular will from tail to flattened triangular head, and he writhed, kneading forward coil to coil, all the while drilling the air with his tongue, his breath thinned to a narrow hiss as he wrinkled and unwrinkled himself along the tree. Minutes went by, then hours, as he inched farther up the incline. Midway, he looked down to see that his entire body was now above the surface of the pool.

At last he reached the crown of the toppled tree, where foot- and hand-holds presented. Only then did the water snake slide from the tree trunk and ascend along the secondary branches to become once more a man. Nolan climbed until he stood in the highest crotch of the crown with his hands outstretched, holding to branches overhead.

The day was beginning to break. In the faint light he saw that at its nearest the tree was separated from the solid bank of the bog by a distance of some twenty feet. Land! In his heart he shouted the word like one who has been shipwrecked and cast adrift. But to reach that bank he must cross this iron-colored water with its dragging weeds, its quicksand. It is the last test, he thought. But this time his resolve failed him. He could not bring himself to descend again into that bog, where death lay in wait for him. Standing in the crown of the tree, he was like a sailor in high rigging, or some pale tatter that had been snagged. From where he hung in the branches Nolan could see the beginning of the path that wound up to the village, and the neat pile where his clothing lay. Even were he able to master his fear, he knew he would not reach so far but would be pulled down into the quick- sand. And now Nolan knew that the death he had been seeking all these months and no longer wanted would, for all the struggle, be his. The murderous bog would have him. Sorrow overcame him; he was limp with it. Arms spread and clinging to a branch above his head, he let his chin fall to his chest; his knees buckled. The strength flowed from his body. It would not be long, he thought.

From far off Nolan heard a drum of thunder. Soon it would rain, he thought. He waited for a wind, and a wind came. The first mild breath grazed his cheek. His hair lifted at the touch. Another, and another, softly, softly, like the slow respirations of a sleeping man. From somewhere below came the clicking of reeds that had been set into fluctuation by the breeze. Then all was still. And then, a nervous movement, a bristling of leaves and grasses. With the rain, a sudden heave of the wind cuffed him broadside. There was a clatter of twigs breaking, and a thousand pliant grasses wavered, then bent. The bog began to flow again. Then once more all was still.

Abruptly the rumor of storm rose again and now the wind had taken on purpose and mass; the sky darkened. Stronger and stronger came the gusts, so that Nolan had to tighten his grip on the branches overhead. No more the inhalation and exhalation of a great chest, but a tumultuous force, a tempest that bugled in his ears. Shock after shock struck him, knocking the air from his lungs. And with each, his body arched forward, then fell back. Nolan felt the pull of his arms from their sockets, the branches sliding beneath his fingers. Soon there was only the wind. He was blind, deaf, numb with it. He felt himself perfused by wind, felt it passing through his body the way a sail is entered by the wind that drives it, until he was weightless, stripped of nerves and muscles, of all substance, empty of all but the very wind he was becoming. He could not hold on any longer. Now he would let go.

Then there came a mighty blast that tore the tree from his grasp, and Nolan was lifted upward, up and forward, arms outstretched, and catapulted to lie facedown in the glutinous bog, which surged across his back. Wallowing, floundering, his mouth full of sour brine, Nolan felt the tenacious drag of the waterweeds, felt his wrists being cuffed together, his legs trussed. Already he was being pulled down. Choking and blind, he heard above his head the snickering of the bulrushes. All at once, he felt an electric bolt of pain in his right hand that jolted him back into the world. Hearing swung back into his ears; sight slid itself beneath his eyelids. Had he been bitten? Stung? He cried out four times, *Aiee! Aiee! Aiee! Aiee!* shouting the hot vowels of his pain across the bog to the longed-for land beyond his reach. And with each howl he was pulling the pain toward him, to seize and slay it, until, hunching, thrashing, rowing with his left arm and his legs, at last he felt, first beneath his chest and then under his belly and thighs, the hard, firm earth.

A long while later, Nolan opened his eyes. Through a film of mud the naked bog-begotten man saw the blood running down his arm, dripping from his elbow to pool upon the ground. In his right fist he still grasped the clump of sword sedge to which he had unknowingly clamped himself. He opened his hand to release them, and saw the twin jets of blood that spurted from the stump of the finger that the knives of sedge had amputated cleanly where it joined his palm. The webs of his fingers were solid with clot; his palm was screened with blood, his chest and belly enameled with it. He pulled himself to his knees, then upright, gripping his right wrist with his left hand as a tourniquet. As quickly as it had come, as mysteriously, the wind had disappeared, and with it the clouds, leaving behind an empty skin of the moon. In its place there breathed a warm fitful breeze. The sun was shining; overhead, a purity of blue. Nolan lifted his gaze to see the bright sky sparkling with larks. He watched them, one after the other, press themselves into the blue, disappearing into it. Beneath his feet, the earth was dry, solid, warm. How he loved it. The red, the golden morning. Those pardoning larks.

LUIS

... And there fell a great star from heaven, burning as it were a lamp, and
it fell upon the third part of the rivers, and upon the fountains of waters;
And the name of the star is called Wormwood: and the third part of the
waters became wormwood; and many men died of the waters, because
they were made bitter.

Apocalypse 8:10-11

Every morning at precisely eight o'clock—you could set your
watch by him—Arnaldo Cherubini, professor of medicine at the
National University, steps into the black limousine with the bullet-
proof windows and is driven down the mountain to the medical
center, where he is distinguished chairman of the Department of
Radiation Therapy. The road is steep and serpentine that leads
down from the walled and patrolled enclaves where live the great
and wealthy families of the city, protected from the threat of the
unknown. Pedro, the chauffeur, has learned every inch of this road
through the soles of his feet, so often has he driven it.
Unfortunately, now part of the way lies along the northern boundary of the municipal dump. Naturally, Pedro keeps the blue-tinted
windows of the car closed until this area is well past, because of the
smell.

It has not always been a dump. Once, it was the municipal park,
El Jardim Público, the chief ornament of the city, a vast green
acreage laced with paths and shaded by large trees, among which

87

lay topiary gardens, beds of flowers, and, at the center, a white bandstand, all gifts of the foundation established with the fortune built by the professor's grandfather, the mining tycoon Martim Cherubini. But with the bloating of the city and a daily ocean of garbage to be disposed of, it had been decided that a dump was more to the point. For weeks, there had been pious expressions of regret by the government, outrage in the newspapers, but in the end, the citizenry had bowed its head. What else was there to do? And so, with steam shovels and bulldozers, the beautiful belly of the city was gouged open until there was an excavation to a depth of fifteen feet. All but a handful of the ornamental trees where cut down. Even the ancient sundial, which Cherubini's men had commandeered in Bolivia and brought home in triumph, tumbled before the earth movers. For some days, it lay half sunken, with time frozen on its face, then disappeared beneath the surface. By the time the mistake was discovered, no one knew where it was. Even before the digging was finished, the first trucks arrived with their loads of rejectimenta—old tires, shattered glass, plastic containers, and, from a city grown rich and profligate, sprung sofas, rancid carpets, automobiles, refrigerators, and a jumble of dismantled machinery.

In time, the city recoiled from this ulceration at its center, sending suburbs, sinuous and leafy, up into the canyons. The distance one lived from the dump became the measure of one's good fortune. Should a tactless visitor mention the site, a citizen will shrug, give an ironic smile, and say: "Aha! So you have seen our beautiful park."

Any map of the dump would be useless, for each day it is molded anew by the giant earth movers. Yesterday's path has vanished, leaving no trace; what was then a towering mound will have been flattened. Even the margins shift and stretch from day to day, as the dump bites another mouthful from the flank of the city. A listing of the flora and fauna would be more reliable. Only a single species of tree exists here. Stunted and tumorous, it grows root-heavy below its bare, ruined superstructure. Nourished by decay, and less vulnerable than leaves to the poisonous fumes, these roots arch from the ground with a monstrous vitality. Sometimes, when the underground fires burn close, these trees claw at the ground and flail their branches in a kind of histrionic woe. Giant weeds spring up overnight, huge whorish flowers that bloom briefly and die, their generative parts waxy and smelling of vomit.

As for creatures, there are rats, of course, flies, mosquitoes, and pale butterflies. A pack of wild dogs roam here, and solitary cats, each one bearing its unique pattern of scars and fresh wounds. Vultures, gulls, and crows throng the air; here and there the surface undulates with carpets of maggots. And hunkering amid the strands of brownish smoke are the human scavengers, each with a burnt-out cigarette in the corner of his mouth.

A ceaseless gray ash from the fires drifts through the air. Now and then a bit of hot ash falls on the bare back of a digger, causing him to cry out. What with these glowing flakes, the fireflies that abound, and the stars in the sky, it is no wonder that the night scavengers (scavenging is forbidden during the day when the trucks are unloading) are afflicted with a strange confusion. At dawn, when they emerge, they have the dazzled look of men who have undergone a long bombardment. All during the day, the garbage trucks grind in slow lines. An endless evacuation of the waste of the city, an endless replenishment of the smoldering landscape. A muddy path leads away from the dump. At all times it bears the imprint of bare feet, wagon wheels, and the hooves of donkeys. This is the way taken by the scavengers to and from the *favela*, a vast strew of ramshackle huts veined by alleys that are little more than open sewers, every doorway emitting the same stench of excrement, urine, and rotting vegetation. This *favela*, no less than the dump, is deplored by those citizens who look down upon it from the roof gardens of their mountain fortresses. To them it is a scabby rash that creeps up the hillsides. From the same vantage, the dump at night, with its points of light that are the kerosene lanterns of the scavengers, resembles a remote, sleeping village. Should Professor Cherubini point his telescope in that direction, it might seem to him that the scavengers are acting with some colonial purpose, but it is not so. Each of them works alone. Even when they crowd onto a freshly dumped heap, they maintain the aloofness of snakes in a nest who crawl over, under, and around each other without the least sign of recognition. Being a man of cultivation and science, the professor is apt to ponder the phenomenon. More than begging, stealing, or prostitution, it seems to him, scavenging is the rudimentary act of civilized life, as the scavenger requires no presence but his own, and he acts without sense of past or future, with neither superstition, faith, or mercy. To be a scavenger, Dr. Cherubini has decided, is to have reached bottom.

▼   ▼   ▼

On any given night, Luis Figueira can be found at the dump. From a distance, there is nothing to distinguish him from the hundreds of other boys who swarm out of the *favela* to beg, steal, or sell their bodies to the gringo tourists. Closer up, you would see that he is of mixed blood—Indian and Portuguese. It is the Indian that predominates, in the small triangular head, aquiline nose, and pointed chin. A butterfly of dark freckles crosses his face, as though in the mixing of his blood, the pigment had been unevenly scattered. He is of small stature, with slightly bowed legs. If you guess his age at seventeen, you would be a year or two shy of the truth. Like the others, he wears tattered blue jeans, a T-shirt of no recognizable color, and a bandanna tied about his neck. Even his name would not precisely identify him, for doubtless there are ten thousand Luis Figueiras in Brazil, many, it would be safe to say, of mixed Indian and Portuguese blood with amber-colored skin and a crop of black hair.

Seven years ago, Luis left the village of Araguaia, a cluster of houses with its back to the rain forest and facing a great river. The whole village was elevated on wooden stilts, lest the river overflow its banks. For years the transport of rubber and bananas supported the town, but Luis's father was a potter. The boy's earliest memories are of his father's large brown feet working the treadle, his thumbs hollowing out a spinning ball of clay. Now and then, he would pause to ladle water from a bucket to soften the mass or slice away a strip of excess with his knife, all the while humming the half dozen songs with which he accompanied himself and which, he told Luis, made the bowls and jars lighter, gave them rhythm. Sometimes he would reach out a muddy arm and pull Luis onto his lap, show him how to guide the shapeless mass into a bowl with his fist. Each time, it seemed to Luis, his father had performed a miracle. When the pots had been glazed and baked, his mother would take them to the dock to sell to the missionaries and tourists passing through. One day, it was understood, Luis would become a potter too.

But when Luis was twelve, his father stopped humming. The buzz of the wheel was punctuated by a cough. The phlegm on the ground was red.

One day, his mother returned from the dock breathless with excitement. From her basket she drew a crucifix for which she had traded six of the bowls. It had been carved by an Indian from the gnarled wood of a jungle vine. The tortuous grain of the vine was incorporated in the torso of Christ. It was brown and yellow and smooth from handling. The face of Christ was thin and triangular like the faces of the Indians. His hair was long and dark. His head drooped upon a narrow chest in which each rib was visible; about his waist, an elaborate loincloth. As the girth of the vine had not been great, a portion of the crossbar was missing, and the arms ended in jagged stumps. Luis had never seen anything so sad or so beautiful. His mother hung it on the wall. Often, it was the last thing he saw before falling asleep.

The rubber trade dwindled, and with it the river traffic that had sustained the village. For the first time, Araguaia knew hunger. One by one, Luis's brothers and sisters left for the cities to find work, until only he was left at home.

"I will send for you in time," each of them had promised. But he never heard a word.

For six months, his father lay on a woven mat beneath the crucifix, coughing and strangling, and filling the house with the smell of rotting flesh. The other villagers hurried by, holding cloth over their noses and mouths, but still the stench seeped into their skin. Señor Figueira died before he had passed on his craft to his son, but not before he had bequeathed to him his illness. When Luis's cough persisted, his mother took him down the river to another village from which a path led into the jungle. In a thatched hut, an old Indian woman drew him toward the chair where she sat as on a throne. She pressed her ear to his chest, her hair rancid under his chin. When she had heard enough she left the room, returning with a small slate-colored pouch from which she took a bowl of hard black gum. This she heated over a flame until it was soft, then kneaded and rolled it until it was a flattened disk, which she pasted over his left nipple.

"He will cough for half as long a time as he has lived," said the old woman. "Then he will cough no more."

One day, Luis's mother lay down on the mat where his father had died and did not rise again. It took her two weeks of hard struggle to die. "Mamá! Mamá!" Luis called out to her, but she did not answer. Only when he coughed would she, out of some vestige of maternal anxiety, turn her head to him. When she died, Luis took the crucifix from the wall and placed it in her hand. Afterward, a handful of old men and women came to help bury her.

"What about that?" An old woman pointed to the crucifix.

"Let it go with her," said Luis. A week later, he stood on the deck of a small launch, gazing at his receding village. In return for his passage to the city he was to load and unload the cargo of beans.

Arnaldo Cherubini looks every bit the distinguished professor. Dona Hortênsia sees to that. His silver hair is punctually trimmed, as are his beard and moustache, although in recent years, much to his wife's dismay, he has permitted himself a bit of shagginess around the mouth. But then, his eminence allows for it. Dona Hortênsia is proud of her husband's appearance. His suits are of the finest fabrics, and perfectly cut. His shoes, handmade abroad, are all but weightless and of such a softness as to suggest that the leather had been chewed for days by Italian workmen. All this he wears with a natural grace, as though it were an elegant hide inside which his body, whatever its imperfections, might move with ease.

Thirty years ago, when the time had come to choose which field of medicine he would pursue, Arnaldo Cherubini had at once decided on radiology. It had been a brilliant, albeit natural, selection. For from childhood he was possessed of an innate fastidiousness that caused him to step back, to recoil even, from the unlovely facts of the flesh—the way it snorted, spat, sweated, defecated, putrefied. The X-ray beams stripped the body of its distasteful functions as of all its superfluities, and so redeemed it in his eyes. To be a radiologist, he decided, was congenial to his instrument, and he had never once regretted his choice.

There is no doubt in the mind of Dona Hortênsia that her husband is a genius.

"Everything in Arnaldo," she is fond of saying, "is in balance. He sees things that the rest of us cannot see. But then . . ." and here she shakes her head and gives a musical laugh, "he has always been refined. I think he was born refined. I cannot imagine what could take away his dignity."

If Arnaldo Cherubini has one shortcoming, it is his devotion to tobacco. "The fumes of learning," he calls it. To the sorrow of his colleagues and the dismay of his students, he persists in this vile habit, shrugging off their dire prophecies.

"All this nagging," he retorts. "It cannot possibly be good for anyone. It is worse than a little tobacco." A little! Were you to be admitted to his office at the university, or chance to be invited to his rooftop garden, you would see him enveloped in an aromatic cloud. "Like Zeus on Mount Olympus," as Dona Hortênsia puts it. "Sometimes, Arnaldo," she said to him once, flicking her little ivory fan to clear the air, "sometimes, I think you make all this smoke so that I cannot find you. You like to hide in it."

Truth to tell Dona Hortênsia is worried about her husband, but it has nothing to do with his smoking. He so rarely smiles these days.

▼   ▼   ▼

For the first two years Luis lived on the streets of the *favela*, one of a horde of homeless, half-starved children, each one longing for the village left behind. Even the meanest, most malarial hometown became a paradise in their memories. For an Indian boy alone in the city, the choices are few. Initially, Luis had gone begging. Even with his small size and the cough that he learned to use to advantage, there were seldom enough coins at the end of the day to buy something to eat. After some months, he joined one of the street gangs who, in groups of three or four, slit open the purses of the gringos or jostled the men while picking their pockets. But in stealing, a cough was not an asset. More than once he had spoiled a robbery. Twice he had been caught and beaten by police. Afterward, the other boys had turned on him angrily.

One evening, when he had had nothing to eat for days, and clawed at his belly as though the hunger were a thing he could rip out, he had gone down to the beachfront lined with tourist hotels. He had learned from the others how it was done; you stand in a place where you are sure to be seen, but in the shadows, not in the open. When a gringo looks, you look back. When he nods, you nod in return. Always do it outdoors, on the beach, in the bushes. Never go to his room. Trembling against a palm tree, Luis waited.

It was only his body, after all. A man appeared, walked by, looked. Luis looked back. The man nodded; Luis nodded. Minutes later, when the man reappeared, Luis steeled himself. But in the end, he had cried out in pain and the man, in disgust, had slapped him hard. Luis would not go there again. He would rather starve. That left only the dump.

From the beginning, Luis was strangely drawn to the dump. Somehow it reminded him of the jungle that pressed against Araguaia, fecund and dangerous. But in the forest the dense canopy of treetops holds your thoughts down below. The dump is a jungle with its lid torn away.

Should you descend into the dump at night, you would find Luis among the other scavengers, squatting by his lantern, his bare feet sunk to the ankles, his hands thrust beneath the surface, working, working. If the stench is nauseating, Luis does not acknowledge it. He has long since become inured to it, as he has to the rats and the flies with which he competes. Only when the baying dogs draw near do his armpits itch, for he has never lost his fear of them. To Luis, they are the devils of the dump. Now and then, to his relief, the guards, stationed there to prevent scavenging during the day when the trucks are unloading, will shoot the whole pack out of boredom. Then you can see their half dozen carcasses mantled by the wings of vultures. Within days, other dogs have found their way to the place; a new pack forms.

Luis sits on his heels more comfortably than he once sat in a chair. Early on, he discovered that he had the feet for it—flat, squelchy, Indian feet with which to ride the swiveling dump. The trick is to ride the inner boil as if it were the deck of a ship. More than once he has pulled himself up by ropes of air. From nightfall to daybreak hunger narrows his focus. Hour after hour he sifts with his fingers or digs with the short hoe that, along with his lantern and a small makeshift wagon, are the tools of his trade. His fingers grow raw from the moisture. Now and then, he holds up to the lantern a dripping possibility, then lets it fall. Only a week before, driven by hunger, he had tried to steal into the dump before dark and had been chased by the guards. His ribs are still sore from their blows. On the night that you see him, he has found only a few spoiled oranges. But then—what luck!—a paper plate to which a paste of beans has stuck. He eats it, plate and all. Still, it is surprising what one can find here that might be traded or even sold.

When one of the ever-burning fires engulfs a rubber tire, the already putrid air turns thick as jelly and settles in his chest so that he must give in to the cough that shakes him as though he were a bundle of sticks. Now and then a fight breaks out. Two of the scavengers leap toward each other, cursing, snarling. Fists are raised, knives drawn. Over and over they roll, thumping, slashing, until rage is spent. Or is it rage? Perhaps they are like cats under the pull of estrus who must mate no matter what. Luis knows that one day he, too, will have to fight. The scavenger who turns from such a challenge is as good as lost. From his thieving days Luis has kept the knife he used to slash the women's purse straps. He wears it in a straw sheath at his belt.

For a long time, Luis was plagued by homesickness. Again and again, in his mind, he ran through all the old familiar losses: the death of his parents, the departure of his brothers and sisters. He could not stop thinking of the villagers, who were so used to one another that when they spoke in their careless quick dialect, no stranger could understand them; how their sentences had no beginning or end but were a continuation of what had been said yesterday and what would be said tomorrow.

In time, the garrulous old ghosts were still. He no longer heard their sweet jabbering. The dump had become his village, and hunger brooks no rivals. Besides, he had become a stargazer. Among whatever crowd of burrowers in the earth, there is always the one who will lift up his eyes. Such a one is Luis. Many nights in Araguaia his father had pointed to the night sky and shown him there the jaguar, the scorpion, the giant tortoise. Now, night after night, he sends his fingers blindly into the earth and his gaze to the teeming sky. For Luis, it is charged with meaning, a great page of hieroglyphs that he never tires of reading. There, directly overhead, is the bent hook like the one on which his father hung the ladle for wetting down the clay. And there, nearby, the ladle itself. Farther away he sees the flock of parakeets forever about to fly over the rim of the sky. But then the sky changes, and the flock of parakeets turn into a woman who pursues her one-legged husband. Another time, in the same place, he sees a tapir making love to a woman. It is almost as though each night he creates the sky with his eyes.

Nights of discovery. Hour by hour his right arm goes on by itself with a mechanical intelligence of its own. Now and then, he switches the hoe to his left hand, then back again. Always just beneath the surface there is something unformed and invisible waiting to be found: bird bones, chunks of animals, rotting fruit—everything gnawed and ripped. Once, he had followed a descent of gulls to a large plastic bag. In a moment it had been beaked open, spilling fetuses. Two things he has found that he keeps—a fragment of a bowl exactly like the ones his father made, and a flute. The flute is carved of wood, part of what had once been a set of pan-pipes. When he unplugged the four note holes, he blew into it and was startled at the sweetness of the notes—hollow and reverberant, as though they came from far away. He does not dare part with it. For all his years of street life, Luis still endows certain objects with hidden power. One day, shortly after he turned eighteen, he was playing the flute when he felt something dislodge deep within his chest, as though a stone had been rolled away. All at once his mouth filled with a sour fluid, which, leaning forward on his elbows, he let flow to the ground. On and on it flowed and all the while Luis felt the tightness in his chest lifting as though a wire band had been unwound from about his body. When at last he had spat the last of it, he inhaled deeply, easily, he for whom no single breath in six years had been free.

Each morning Luis pulls his wagon from stall to stall in the marketplace of the *favela*, offering what he has found—an umbrella with two broken struts, a straw hat with a torn brim, a plastic vase still holding a few artificial flowers. One day he caught sight of a woman begging in a corner of the marketplace. In one arm she held a baby at her breast. Another child slept across her lap, and a third sat on the ground playing with pebbles. It was a moment before he saw that the woman was his sister Clara.

That night, Clara told him how she had left Araguaia by boat, then walked for many days until she was picked up by a truck driver. It was the truck driver's cousin Ramón whom she had married. Well, not really married. She told him how two years before, Ramón had left for Amazonia to find work. She had not heard any word in that time.

Luis and Clara sized each other up. There was a great open sore on Clara's ankle; she had lost many teeth. An old woman of twenty-four.

Since then Luis has been sleeping on a mat on the floor of her hut. What with Clara's begging and his scavenging, the children have something to eat.

▼　　▼　　▼

After many hours, Luis has found six tin cans, a plastic bottle such as is used to carry kerosene, a small wooden crate. Nothing to eat. In the sky he has found the heart-shaped vulture, its head drawn down into its neck. It is summer and the great tortoise has crawled into the southern sky. The hot, dry time has begun. Toward morning, a wind takes the fire so that flags of flame fly from the trees, lizards of it slithering on the heaps. Among the drifting smoke move the dark, indistinguishable shapes of the scavengers. Their spittle sizzles where it falls. A rat jumps up and bites its own scorched leg. Even on a night like this, the flowers cannot be kept from erupting in violent blooms of purple, orange, red.

All at once, Luis hears a hoarse sawing cry that is not that of an animal. There is too much despair in it. A wake of silence follows.

Perhaps he has imagined it? But then comes the low growling of dogs. A hundred, two hundred yards Luis creeps, until he hears the sound of flesh ripping, the cracking of bones. Closer still he draws, then sees by the light of his upheld lantern a circle of bloody snouts tugging sideways against each other. It was an old woman, he sees, with gray hair and gold hoops in her ears. Her nose and lips are gone but the eyes, open and staring, give back to him his own horrified stare; the dogs had not waited. It is daybreak when they finish. A vulture flaps down to take up the feast. When Luis swipes at it with his hoe, the bird hops to one side. One of the earrings lies alongside what had been her head, embedded still in a bit of flesh. He cuts it free with his knife. For a long time, despite the daylight, Luis stays to comb the remains but he cannot find the other earring. For a week, he, Clara, and the children eat well.

▼   ▼   ▼

One night, Luis digs in a mound of new garbage. On the other side work two older men and a younger, whom Luis has seen in the *favela*. His name is Manuel. When Luis hears him calling out "Monkey!" and "Son of a whore!" he knows. A plum of burning embers lands at his feet, then Manuel emerges, his eyes glittering under pitch-black brows. Luis's heart gives a sickening lurch before he makes it go still as a stone in his chest. Only the hoe in his hand continues to rise and fall, like a watch that goes on ticking in the pocket of a dead man. Into the terrible stillness a bottle is hurled that explodes into a galaxy about him. The sharp wetness on his thigh is his own blood. His knife leaps from belt to hand, the hilt sticky in his fist as he rises to greet his challenger. Even in his fear, he marvels at the young man's head, which is like a knob of excellent wood carved and polished. All at once, Manuel throws back his head and gives a hoarse shout. Abruptly the two close upon each other. Each grabs the wrist of a knife-holding hand. With the other, they punch, pull hair. The blows are dull and painful. Now they are down. Over and over they roll, their hard legs entwined, kicking, kneeing, butting with their heads so as to break a rib, trying to stay out of reach of teeth. At the last, it is Luis who is astride. With all his might, he manages the wrist of the other toward a smoldering ember. He sees Manuel's face dissolve in a grimace of pain, hears him whimper. When Luis sees the knife fall to the ground, he leaps up and out of reach. There is pain in the eyes of the other but no fight left. It is over. Trembling, Luis sheathes his knife and walks away. He will not have to fight again. Weeks later, he will pass Manuel in an alley of the *favela*. They will look at each other shyly, with the tiniest snake of a smile, as though they have shared some shameful secret.

▼   ▼   ▼

In the twenty years of his tenure at the National University Hospital, Arnaldo Cherubini has conducted his country into the era of modern radiation therapy. His department has become the standard against which all other hospitals must be measured. And thanks to Cherubini tin and emeralds, the entire university has flourished. Students and scientists have gathered to study at the feet of the professor and his colleagues. No request for new equipment is denied, and no sooner does a piece of machinery become outmoded, however slightly, than it is discarded and replaced by a newer model. For the professor himself there is nothing but affection and even reverence. Nor has such prestige robbed him of a measure of modesty. He likes to think of himself as just another doctor. Should he so express himself amid the orchestration of lights, crystal, ice, and jewelry at one of his wife's fetes, Dona Hortênsia will smile warmly at her guests and say, "Professor Cherubini has both the kingly and the common touch."

From his days as a medical student in Baltimore, where, amid a sea of poverty, he and his fellows learned their trade on the bodies of charity patients, he has retained the quaint idea that suffering is as much the child of poverty as is evil. Still, he forgives his friends and neighbors their small insensitivities in favor of the pleasure of their company.

At night the professor has taken to observing through his telescope the scavengers at the dump, their lanterns distant as the stars. By the time he steps into the darkened limousine each morning, they have departed for the day.

One morning, he sees through the tinted window a young man just inside the boundary of the dump, pulling a wagon piled high with tin cans. Impulsively, he presses the button to lower his window. As the limousine passes him, the young man—a boy, really—glances up, and the eyes of the two meet for an instant before they are torn apart by the foot of the chauffeur on the accelerator. Arnaldo Cherubini wonders whether the tin in those cans was taken from one of the Cherubini mines.

▼   ▼   ▼

After years of silence, Ramón has come back from Amazonia. Or most of him. One leg is missing. One day he simply appears in the doorway of the hut and swings himself through on his crutches. When he sees the infant lying in the arms of the oldest child, he sucks in his breath, lets one crutch fall to the floor, raises his hand, and brings it down across Clara's face. Luis, awakened by the noise, leaps up, kicks away the remaining crutch, and watches his brother-in-law fall.

"I shall work," he says. "And you shall eat."

After a long silence, the man on the floor nods. "Rum," he says.

▼   ▼   ▼

Once again the giant tortoise has crept into the southern sky. A terrible drought has descended upon the city. For weeks Luis has pulled an empty wagon back to the *favela*. At the dump the fires rage out of control. He has burned the soles of his feet. All through the night, hoeing, hoeing, as if to uncover a new way of life, he watches the wings of birds parting the smoke. Here and there he sees the folded body of one of them on the ground like a sealed envelope.

Already the children of the *favela* have begun to starve. After two days of vomiting blood, Vittorio, Clara's second child, has died. For the first time, Luis has doubts that his scavenging will sustain them. He himself is weak from lack of food. Still he goes nightly to the dump, which roars and throbs like the hot oily hull of a riverboat. More and more, the scavengers resemble the scrawny contorted trees. Only the sky is the same.

One night the sky is alive with shooting stars. Luis watches them dart and vanish like the fish in the river of Araguaia when a net has been thrown—a flash, then afterward a moment of radiance. All at once, he sees that one of the stars does not blink out, but bursts free in a great curving arc. Brighter and brighter it grows, and nearer, as though it has plunged through the sky. Now it is so close that Luis can see the wake of its blazing tail. The sky is charged with meaning, alive with messages that concern him. With each breath he takes, the whole canopy of heaven billows about him. He is plunging too, from one world to another. Perhaps he will faint.

When Luis opens his eyes, he sees at his feet a glowing disk, all about it a pale cloud of light. Kneeling, he takes it up into his hands, and the hairs of light stream between his fingers. The dump sucks at his feet, moving him where it will. Above it, he towers like a soul rising. He looks up at the community of stars from which this one has fallen. To him! To Luis the scavenger! And he falls to his knees and gives thanks to whatever had lifted aside the veil of heaven and cast it down.

When at last the spell is broken, it is as though Luis has awakened from a deep dream of peace. In the sky, the moon, the stars are paling. The star in his hand is also fading. Luis unties the bandanna from around his neck and wraps the star in it. Looking about to see if he has been watched, he goes to one of the trees, kneels to scoop the muck from beneath its arching roots, places the star deep among them, then covers it up again. He will tell no one what has taken place, what he has found. This, if nothing else, will belong to him alone. Hope fills his heart. In the afternoon, it begins to rain. The drought has broken.

The next evening, Luis runs all the way to the dump. At the tree, he drops to his knees, slides his hand among the grappling roots. It is there! Drawing it forth, he is amazed anew at the strange brilliance that turns his amber skin to deep violet. To the left and right of him, the dump is blue in the lesser moonlight. Holding the star to himself, does he imagine that his chest grows warm from its touch?

A month goes by. Time and again, Luis leaves off his digging to unearth the star hidden at the base of the tree. How it pulsates with the rhythm of his own heartbeat. When his eyes have had their fill, he replaces it and returns to his labor. The star will see to his needs, he is sure.

▼   ▼   ▼

One day, as Luis makes one last visit to the hiding place, he sees a guard watching him through field glasses. The guard calls out to another guard, to whom he hands the glasses. From the distance he sees their heads move in conversation. His hiding place has been discovered. He wraps the star, in the bandanna, and places it in the wagon beneath the bottles and tin cans. Slowly, so as not to rouse suspicion, he leaves, pulling the wagon behind him. The guards do not follow. When night comes, he will find another place to hide the star. But now he must bring it home with him. He will leave it in the wagon, beneath his pile of gleanings. He will not sleep.

At noon, he must leave the hut to relieve himself. When he steps back through the doorway, he sees what the little girl holds. Ramón sees too, and on his face is a look of cunning. Luis lunges for the star, but Ramón has snatched it away with one hand. In the other a knife glistens.

"You must give it back," says Luis, but he knows he has lost the star. A wave of dizziness comes over him, the same vertigo of dislocation he had experienced years before when, from the deck of the riverboat, he had watched his village recede from view.

Within minutes, the news has spread through the *favela*. Soon a crowd has gathered in the open doorway, where Ramón holds up the star for them to see. How bravely it glows in the light of day.

"Block out the light from the door. You will see how brightly it shines." Ramón's face is tight with avarice.

"It is a miracle!"

"A piece! A tiny piece! To save us." And soon there is a line of women at the door. Each hands money to Clara, each holds open a pouch into which Ramón shaves a fragment of the star. The women murmur and cross themselves. In the street, embarrassed and excited, the men stand in groups, smoking and drinking beer. The *favela* is swept by rapture, brims with the seeds of hope.

Hour by hour, Luis watches the star shrink beneath Ramón's knife. Paler and paler it grows, smaller and smaller, until only a handful of dust remains, which Clara scatters about the hut.

"To bring us good fortune," she exclaims, laughing with joy. Ramón closes the door. In the windowless room, the scattered dust gives off a sad glow.

▼　　▼　　▼

At precisely three o'clock on Friday afternoon, Professor Cherubini, in a starched and immaculate coat, enters the auditorium for radiology grand rounds. The students, interns, and residents fall silent. *El Catedrático*, they call him behind his back. A cathedral of a man. Lumbering, as if under the weight of his honors, he makes his way to a chair at the center of the first row, facing a bank of viewing boxes. An intern rises to give a brief résumé of the history, physical findings, and laboratory data of the first case. The lights are turned off. A row of skulls looks down at the conferees from the panel of viewing boxes. Beneath, a second row of skulls gazes to the left like figures in an Egyptian frieze. The patient, it has been explained, has a tumor of the pituitary gland. Dr. Cherubini rises to stand closer to the X-rays, peering, milking an earlobe for thoughts. At last, he motions for the students to draw near. There is a brief subdued hubbub until twenty are grouped about him, each head cocked to catch whatever scraps of wisdom will fall from his lips. The scene has reminded more than one visitor of a painting by Rembrandt. Pointing with a thin gold pencil, the professor shows the erosion of the sella turcica where the expanding tumor has compressed it. Dr. Cherubini resumes his chair. The others do likewise. The CAT scan is then shown, followed by the arteriogram. Here, the professor comments upon the "blush" of abnormal blood vessels, the displacement of the arteries. Last to be shown are the pictures obtained by the use of the Cherubini Foundation's latest gift, a nuclear magnetic resonator. Now the intern tells the number and dosage of radiation treatments and the portals through which they have been delivered. A third panel of viewing boxes is flicked on. These show the post-treatment X-rays. There is no evidence whatsoever of a space-occupying mass. The sella turcica has begun to fill in with new bone. The blood vessels have returned to a normal pattern. The intern relates that the patient no longer suffers double vision, headache, or mental confusion. Her condition appears normal. When the intern has finished his report a self-congratulatory murmur fills the room.

▼   ▼   ▼

It is dusk. Already the moon has risen. Luis is pulling the wagon along the road, scanning for fresh tire tracks that will show him a fresh mound in which to forage. In the month since he has lost the star, he has come to see the dump as the tourists do, as do those who live high on the mountainside. It seems to him the malevolent working intestine of the city and himself no better than a maggot feeding on decay. Each time he looks up at the stars, his grief flares anew for what he was given, for what he has lost.

All at once he is aware of someone standing directly in front of him. Automatically he raises his hands. Then he sees that it is a girl, her gaze turned upward. She might be his own age or younger. Her face seems to have gathered all the moon's light to itself. A shyness comes over Luis. He is on the point of walking on when she speaks.

"How big it is, how close."

"You mustn't stare at it so."

She turns to face him. Has he seen her before? In some alley of the *favela*, squatting over a heap of mangos at the market? He cannot remember, but somewhere is the memory of this milk-and-gray girl.

"Why shouldn't I?"

"The moon can drive you crazy when it's full. Better to look at the stars. You'd be surprised at what you can see." She is either a whore or a witch, he thinks.

"Show me, then. Show me something you see in the stars."

"I don't have time for that. I have to go to work."

"Oh." There is a disappointment in her voice. "Then you must go." So. She is not a whore. A whore wouldn't tell you to go.

Suddenly she gives a low moan and sways. Luis steps forward and catches her about the waist. How frail she is, he notices.

"Are you sick?"

"The smell." She frees herself from his arm.

"Oh, that. I don't notice anymore. Are you all right?"

"It's nothing. I get dizzy from many things."

"Are you hungry?"

"No." But he sees that she is.

"I get dizzy when I look up at the sky," she says.

"That's because you don't know how to do it." He does not want her to leave. "All right, I suppose I can show you. But only one." He turns the wagon into the dump and begins to walk briskly. When she does not follow, he calls back over his shoulder.

"Well, aren't you coming? Or did you change your mind?"

"I can't see," she says. He returns to her.

"Give me your hand." He leads her into the dump. "What's your name?"

"Joana."

"Listen, Joana, I have two potatoes. I will roast them in the fire. One is for you. Meanwhile, we can look at the stars."

A hundred yards into the dump, he stops.

"Here is a good place." She watches in silence while he lights a small fire and sets the potatoes. When he is done, he goes to stand next to her.

"Look there," he points upward. "That is the great hook just like the one in my father's house where he used to hang the ladle."

"You mustn't point at the stars," she interrupts, pressing his hand down. "You'll get a wart on your finger."

"Where did you hear such nonsense? And there, look, is the vulture with its head drawn down into its neck. Why are you squinting? Keep your eyes open."

"I am myopic. I can't see faraway things. It helps to squint." Strands of her hair brush his cheek. "Why is everything in the sky tilted?"

"It is the way you are looking. You have to learn how."

"Show me one more."

He shows her the flock of parakeets. "Five, six, seven, eight. They're going to fly over the rim of the sky."

When she has eaten with gusto and delicacy, she says, "I must go now, but I don't know the way." Once again into his callused palm he takes her smooth tiny hand that life has not coarsened. Together they retrace their steps.

"Why do you come to this horrible place?" she shivers.

"It isn't horrible."

"The smell, everything rotting. The rats."

Luis cannot help laughing. "The rats? They are only trying to stay alive too. I have learned from them how to do it."

"May I come again sometime?"

He looks down at her hands. "The dump is not for you."

"How do you know what is for me?" Her face is young but knowing. She, too, has made her own way, he thinks.

"Do what you want," he says gruffly. "I don't own the dump." Without another word, the girl turns and runs down the path. Luis returns to the wagon. Immediately he begins to sift the garbage with his hands. But on this night, his eyes are full not of the stars but of her luminous image.

The next night she is there, at the same place in the path. She has brought a piece of calico of the same printed pattern as her dress. He watches her fold the square of cloth neatly, again and again, pressing it with her hand until it is a narrow band. Then, standing on tiptoe, she places it about his forehead, tying it at the back. Her bare arms lie along his temples while he stares down at her like an animal that does not know whether it is to be beaten or caressed.

On the third night, he waits for her on the path, swinging his lantern, until with a rush of despair he thinks she is not coming. But then there she is, and he forces himself not to run toward her.

Beneath three trees in a narrow valley among the mounds he has spread a mat for her. She waits, watching his back, the methodical rise and fall of the hoe in his upraised hand, the way a small animal waits to be discovered. Up and down goes the hoe, up and down. At last, he turns toward her. When she lowers her head, a strand of her hair falls forward over her eyes. It is the sign he has been waiting for. He lifts the strand and tucks it behind her ear. Then they are lying together on the mat, listening to the delirium of each other's arms and legs while all about the living earth beats in rhythm with their hearts and they feel between their close-pressed bodies the wings of a moth open and close.

Later, lying behind her, he watches the slow rise and fall of her shoulder as she sleeps. She seems to him full of secrets. In the acute restlessness of his joy, he does not know what to do with himself. He squats to dig with a kind of frenzy, rises to pace back and forth, then, beside himself, he takes out the flute. She is awake, listening. Turning, she sees that his face has taken on an expression like sleep, or as though the sky were passing through him.

▼   ▼   ▼

Before daybreak, Joana leaves to fetch another load of mangos from the country. At the marketplace she will pick her way among the vendors—butchers selling tripe, oxtails, the bloody heads of sheep; women selling hanks of cloth, pots and pans, religious trinkets, cheap rum—until she comes to the open yard thronged with peddlers of fruit and vegetables. She will spread a woven mat on the ground, then wash and set out her mangos. Here she will remain—one day, two, three—until she has sold them or they have spoiled.

Sifting through ashes, Luis feels a buzzing in his fingertips and a strange, not unpleasant heat spreading over his hands as though they have come too near the fire. He holds them to the lantern. Has he been stung? Burned? He scrubs them in the air, then dismisses it from his mind.

But the next night the buzzing is stronger and with it, a feeling of fullness in his fingers as though there were too much blood in them. By daylight he sees that the skin of his hands is pink, shiny, and taut. He cannot close his fists. Twice, the hoe has slipped from his grasp. By the next day, the pain has declared itself. Luis is conscious of the blood streaming through his body, pounding for exit against his swollen fingertips. On the palm of his right hand, a great blister has risen. Pressing it with a finger, he sees fluid moving under his skin. Beneath his touch, the blister breaks; a warm fluid runs across his palm. Luis takes hold of the torn skin and peels it from his hand. What comes off is a glove with two fingers. Alone, he gives in to a conflagration of childlike weeping that burns itself out in sleep, where he is once again in Araguaia, the river flowing cool through him.

Joana has returned. She stares at the moist raw flesh to which already the first flies have been drawn. Together they study the sores that have opened up at the tips of his fingers.

▼   ▼   ▼

With his ruined hands Luis is no match for the rats, dogs, and crows. He envies them their teeth, beaks, and claws. For the first time, he is afraid of the dump.

"Never mind," says Joana. "You will tell me where to dig."

Luis looks down at her small delicate hands and his heart fills with sorrow. "Only until you are all better," she says. "I will not leave you." Now it is she who pulls the wagon and lifts the hoe while Luis sits on his heels, rocks back and forth to the throbbing. By day, they take turns sleeping in the streets of the *favela*.

Within days his hands have begun to smell. The death face of his father returns to him.

"It is no good," she tells her.

"What are you saying? Don't be foolish," she says. But she, too, has smelled the odor of decay, and the words limp unconvincingly from her mouth. At last she cries, and when Luis can bear her sorrow no longer, he tells her of the night of the shooting stars, and how he had not kept his vow to protect what had been given to him.

"Now you see," he tells her, lifting his hands. "I have been punished."

At length she says, "Then I shall be your hands. But first, tomorrow, we must go to the clinic at the hospital, to show the doctors. Perhaps there is a medicine, something to do."

▼   ▼   ▼

In a cubicle of the clinic Luis is sitting on a stretcher. His hands are wrapped in filthy rags tied at the wrists. Joana stands nearby. Between them there is the formality that such situations confer even upon lovers. A nurse peels away the cloths, dousing them with water when they will not come unstuck. Her lips and nostrils are compressed in judgment of the stench of dead tissue. What is laid bare is only black leather, yellow bone, pus. Two doctors come and go, then stop just outside of the cubicle.

"What could have produced those lesions? Wet gangrene. Is it circulatory?"

"No, The pulses are strong and full. Besides, he's only nineteen."

"Burns, then?"

"From what? And both hands?"

"These stupid Indians and their kerosene."

"Perhaps something he picked up at the dump?"

"He won't be rummaging there anymore." The doctors reenter the cubicle. Joana eats them with her eyes.

"We don't know what caused it. Was there anything you might have picked up that could have burned you?" Joana flashes a glance at Luis. When there is no answer, the doctor speaks again.

"You must go now for X-rays. After that, you can go home." He motions for the nurse to dress the wound. "But you must come back tomorrow."

When Luis and Joana have left, the doctors linger in the cubicle.

"They never tell the truth, those *favelados*. It is like practicing veterinary medicine."

▼   ▼   ▼

The next day, Luis and Joana return to the clinic. Outside the doorway, the two doctors are muttering to each other.

"How could this have happened?"

"It must have been tossed out with the old machine, the one Cherubini replaced a couple of months ago. No one thought to remove the cesium. It ended up at the dump, where he found it. God knows how long he's been playing with it. It's just the sort of thing to make a scandal."

"How do you know for sure?"

"When he went for X-rays, the Geiger counter went wild."

"Does Cherubini know?"

"He's on the way over now."

"Here? To the clinic?" The doctors step into the cubicle.

"Well, well, Luis. How do you—" He is stopped by the girl.

"There is something," she says. "Something that he touched." She hesitates.

"What is it? Come on, come on! The professor will be here in a few minutes. Speak!"

"A star," says Joana.

"A star?"

"Yes, a star." Luis flings the word at them with one trembling stump. "I saw it fall from the sky right where I stood. I hid it under a tree and each night I took it out to see how it glowed until . . ."

"Until what?"

"Until one day I had to bring it home because the guards had seen. It was taken away from me and broken into pieces to sell to the others."

"What did it look like, your star?"

"Like a star."

"What shape was it?"

"It had the shape of a star."

The doctors leave. Through the open doorway, Joana and Luis hear them speaking. "Professor," they hear, and "star."

"God knows how many others . . ."

"By now, it is all through the *favela* . . ."

Arnaldo Cherubini enters the cubicle. He wears his immaculate starched white laboratory coat. His mouth seems to have sunk into the nest of gray hair gathered about it. He wears dark-tinted, horn-rimmed glasses. There is about him an air of disguise, as though he were an actor playing the role of a doctor. At the sight of Luis, he starts. Does he remember that brief glance exchanged months before through the window of his car? Or perhaps it is something else that tells him that he has met the one patient who will change his life.

For a long time he stands in silence, looking down at Luis, the knuckles of one fist pressed hard into his beard. Luis feels the man's gaze upon him like a weight pressing him down. Behind the beard and the dark glasses lies something still and rapt. Luis cannot know that with his simple offering of wounds, his appearance is just as marvelous to the doctor as the shooting star had been to him.

At last, Cherubini clears his throat and, with a gesture of immense weariness, reaches up to take off the glasses. A deep crease rises from the bridge of his nose to the middle of his brow as though a nail had been driven into his forehead. He steps closer to the stretcher. The smell rising from the hands brings tears to his eyes.

"Is there much pain?" he asks. Luis looks down at his hands as if imploring them to answer for him. "But surely you can tell me if you have pain," Cherubini urges.

Luis shakes his head wistfully. "Not now. In the beginning, yes. Now they are just . . . dead."

"Look, Luis." The doctor's voice is heavy with regret. "We know what happened to your hands. There has been a terrible accident." And he recounts how one day an old broken machine had been taken out of the hospital to make room for a new one. How inside the old machine was a piece of metal that gives off dangerous rays that kill human flesh. "We use these rays to cure people of tumors. Somehow, when the machine was loaded on the dump truck, the hot metal had been left inside. When the machine was dumped, the metal fell out. That is what you found. It is true that at night the metal glows so that you can see its light. Like a star," he says gently, "but not a star. It is what has burned you."

Cherubini coughs into his fist and motions for the nurse to bandage the boy's hands. "The only thing to do now is to cut here . . . and here." He draws a finger across each of Luis's arms above the elbow. "Where the flesh is healthy and has a chance to heal." At the touch, the stump of the boy's right hand jerks upward in a sudden reflex. The doctor recoils as if threatened with a blow. "They are already dead, Luis. You have said so yourself. The hospital will pay for everything and you will have enough money to live on from now on. I promise you that!"

But the boy has turned to stone. It is the girl who speaks, but only to Luis.

"Come, we will go home now."

Cherubini turns to face her. "I cannot let you do this," he whispers. "As for the star, it was a false enchantment. A dream. I want to make it up to you for . . . it is our . . . it is my fault that this happened. You must let me . . . please?" He feels the corner of his lip twitching. He is certain that it can be seen despite the beard and moustache. He presses his fingers there to still it, but cannot.

Already the pair are making their way across the dusty courtyard thronged with patients. Should one of them happen to look up, he would see in the doorway of the clinic a doctor in a white laboratory coat holding out his hand like someone who is trying to see if it is raining. "Please!" he is calling out. "Please!" He holds on to the word as though it would keep him afloat.

Outside the gates of the hospital, Joana helps Luis into the wagon. She places a straw hat on his head and takes up the handle.

"What does it mean—false enchantment?" Luis asks her.

"It is a lie," she replies. "There is no such thing. About enchantment, you cannot choose."

"I have seen what I have seen," says Luis.

"Don't talk," she says. "Rest."

It is evening when they reach the dump. "Come on," she says. "You will tell me where to dig. You always know the best place." She helps him out of the wagon to sit with his back against a tree. A small wind plays among the twisted branches, and Luis, too, trembles. In and out of the pocket of moonlight in which they are huddled, a huge ghost-colored moth is floating. From somewhere comes an angry gabbling and the thump of vultures buffeting each other with their wings.

"What are you thinking?" she asks him.

"Thinking?"

"Tell me."

"I was thinking . . . it is not wise to become too attached to your hands. One day they may be taken away from you."

When she sees that he has fallen asleep she takes up the hoe and begins to turn the earth, singing softly to herself. Hours later, he awakens with a start.

"How long have I been asleep?"

"Long enough."

They speak no longer of the past or the future, as though they have agreed that there is only the present. Again and again, Luis tries to remember what had been the last act, the last gesture of his hands. It seems as important to remember this as it would be to remember the last words of the dying.

▼   ▼   ▼

It is midsummer. The tempo of the dump quickens. The ground heaves with the larvae of insects. Luis's left arm ends in an ulcerated black knob at the wrist; the right is an open shaft from which a dry yellow bone protrudes. Swallowing has become painful. When he stands, colored lights flash behind his eyes. His ears are full of whispers. More and more his dreams are of Araguaia. The river shivers, the nets are shaken out. *"Pull, Luis! Pull!"* cry his brothers. From a doorway, his father's voice rises with a song, then stops. Already his memories are scampering off like rats. Overhead, vultures turn like the hands of a clock.

"It won't be long," he tells Joana.

"You must drink," she says. From the market she has brought a pint of rum. She cradles his head, lifts it to his lips.

He is fully awake now, lucid. "Listen, Joana. When the time comes, you must take the hoe, dig a deep hole, and put me there."

She covers her mouth and looks away. With effort, Luis hitches himself closer to her.

"You must promise. Do you promise?"

"How will I know when it is time?" Her voice is barely audible, tired. "I have never seen anyone die before."

"When you can't see your reflection in my eyes anymore. That will be the last thing." He reaches out to stroke her face, then remembers. It is hard to break the habit of hands; they go on reaching for things.

▼　　▼　　▼

Once again it is time for the radiology grand rounds. From the majesty with which Arnaldo Cherubini enters and takes his seat in the front row, you could not know that he has spent the night prowling his rooftop garden, now and then pausing to peer through the telescope at the dump with its many points of light that are as remote from him as the stars. But in the middle of the presentation of the first case, he rises and, without a word, leaves the room.

Under the pretext of persistent headache, Cherubini has asked his chief technician to take an X-ray of his head. He is not to mention this to anyone. Now the professor sits alone in his locked office before a bank of viewing boxes that illuminate the image of his own skull. He does not see the cranial suture lines, the zygomatic arches, the styloid processes, any of the other anatomical features. What he sees, gazing deep into the orbital sockets, is the nakedness of it. It is as though he is looking at the death that lies hidden beneath his skin, only waiting to be released. "You have lived too long among X-rays," he says aloud to the skull.

It is three days since he watched Joana and Luis leave the clinic. For three days he has waited for them to return. During this time, men in lead-lined suits and gloves have fanned out through the *favela*, holding up Geiger counters that tick loud and soft, loud and soft, in accordance with a will of which the people have no inkling. Only when they see their houses nailed shut and plastered with skull and crossbones do they suspect. No one knows how many have been rounded up. Trucks equipped with megaphones have cruised the alleys, calling out, "Diarrhea, vomiting, bleeding from the mouth, loss of hair, sores, loose teeth . . ." But who doesn't have one or two of these? Probably it is just another trick by the government to take from them the little that they have. Let them go to hell.

For three days Arnaldo Cherubini has waited. He can wait no longer. He flicks off the viewing box and presses the button on his desk to notify Pedro that he is ready to leave. It will take the chauffeur five minutes to bring the car to the door of the hospital.

At half past four, Pedro pulls the limousine to the side of the road and opens the rear door.

"Wait here for me. It will be some time. Do not look for me. I will come when I am ready." The chauffeur cannot hide his puzzlement. The doctor silences him with a wave of his hand.

"Do as you are told," he says, though not unkindly. Then he turns toward the dump. In a moment he has disappeared down the embankment. Pedro sighs and lights the first of many cigarettes.

Slowly, for the muck drags at his feet, Arnaldo Cherubini makes his way among the heaps. From time to time the stench causes him to retch and cover his mouth. He makes no effort to brush away the flies clouding about him. Now and then, he pauses to turn a bit of refuse with the toe of his shoe, bends to examine it, then moves on.

He remembers the park that had been the pride of the city. Now, in those colorless mounds and puddles, the whole of the hideous topography, he sees only a menacing X-ray of the grottoes, lawns, hedges, and avenues that were once the beautiful Jardim Público. It seems to him now the very delta of hell. Soon, the thin delicate soles of his shoes are slick with garbage. Twice he stumbles. Awkward and huffing, one hand braced against a stunted tree, he pulls the laces of his shoes, pries them off, then his socks. He feels the dump seethe beneath his toes. With a sudden raucous mewing, a flight of gulls lifts, circles once, then descends to a new site. A rat scampers. At some distance, a fire is smoldering. When a breeze takes the smoke and blows it toward him, he must take quick shallow breaths. Time itself has slowed, become viscous. Wherever he looks he sees the same fever-dark eyes in an amber-colored face, and that girl—like a battered bag that one would throw away.

Day into night, and now the dump is fully awake. At first only the crests are lit, then minute by minute the great heaps brighten until moonlight seeps deeper into the craters of the earth. Through the soles of his feet, Cherubini feels how it rises and falls as if in respiration.

From the top of a mound, El Catedrático looks down and sees the hundred lanterns, sees dimly the shapes of men squatting, their hands threshing, scattering. For a moment he stands between the stars and the lanterns, which confuse, waver, melt, and flow one into the other so that he loses all sense of up and down. What time is it? he wonders. He takes the watch from his vest pocket and sees that it has stopped. He descends. The air is silky with bats. Underfoot, the dump sighs and streams.

Dawn is coming, the first faint acidity of it. X-ray time, full of shadows dark and light that illuminate without pity the whole of human misery. Within minutes, the tip of the mountain is bright with sun. The professor stirs and shivers. All at once, a wave of horror comes over him. Blindly he staggers toward the road, where the limousine is waiting. Dimly, he hears the soft growl of the motor, feels himself being borne away.

▼　　▼　　▼

In another part of the dump sits Joana. Luis's body, silvered by the moon, lies across her lap, head upon her arm. But for the fine grain of her lips, the tiny bubbles between her white teeth, the way her fingers climb the rungs of his ribs, pausing to knead the meager flesh as though to create something, the two might be a carving in gleaming wood. A jaguar of dappled light stalks the shadows. Through the fleshless chest, she watches the heart beating itself out. Each time the eyes float out of reach, she coaxes them back with her own unwavering gaze. At last she feels a slight movement of the head. Luis opens his mouth as if to speak, or yawn.

"What?" she whispers, then sees the light receding slowly from his eyes. It seems to her that their last vision is not of her but of something over her shoulder in the sky. Turning to follow his gaze, she sees just below the handle of the bent hook a cluster of four stars, faint but brightening as she looks. She squints to sharpen the focus. There are three stars in a triangle, with a fourth held somewhat apart. Like a hoe in the upraised hand of a small figure, crouching.

POE'S LIGHT-HOUSE

My name is John Jacob Moran. There would be no reason that the world should take cognizance of me—more than of any other poor young house doctor—had it not been given to me thirty years ago to preside over the death of Edgar Allan Poe. On the third of October in the year 1849 a man by that name was placed under my care at Washington Hospital in Baltimore. The patient presented in critical condition. The cold sweat with which he was drenched, his pallor, the wild tremor of his limbs, the hallucinations in which he conversed with imaginary creatures on the walls, and the odor of alcohol on his breath bespoke the diagnosis of acute alcoholic intoxication with delirium. All this is a matter of record and can be confirmed by reference to the hospital charts written by me thirty years ago. I shall not revisit here the wreckage of the body of Edgar Allan Poe. What is not known is that during the five days of my attendance upon the patient, each one marked by toxic madness and stupor, there were brief episodes of utter clarity in which the poet spoke to me of his enslavement to drink, his dashed hopes, the loss of love, and, in a voice full of bitterness, of having betrayed his art. During one such interval, while I sat at the bedside, he told me that, only days before, he had begun to write a new tale called "The Light-house." At the mention of the title, his face took on a glow of reverie as though he had once again caught up the thread of his story. But in a moment the glow had vanished and was replaced by a look of profound sorrow.

"Now, never to be written," he cried aloud. In an effort to distract the man from his torment and in hopes of lifting his spirits, I asked him to tell me the story. For several minutes he lay silent, eyes closed. He seemed to me to be rummaging through the wild tangle of his thoughts. At last, he gave a deep sigh and began to speak.

"'The Light-house,'" he said, "By Edgar Allan Poe." Unbeknownst to him, I had motioned to a nurse to bring paper, ink, and pen, for it was my thought to take down the story as he spoke it so that should he by some divine intervention recover, he would be able to complete the manuscript. Should he fail to recover, the world would have this last outpouring of his genius. And so for the space of a quarter of an hour he spoke; and so I wrote. At the end of which, I looked up to see that he had drifted into a peaceful sleep. It was a sleep from which Edgar Allan Poe was not to awaken. Two days later he was dead.

That, as I have said, was thirty years ago. In the three decades that have followed I have attended the last illness of many hundreds of patients, all of whose agonal suffering I have let slip from my memory. It is only to the deathbed of Edgar Allan Poe that I have felt myself summoned time and again as if by the restless whispering of his soul; summoned as well to the fragment of the story that I who have not at all a literary cast of mind now feel compelled by a will other than my own to complete. For where is it written that the ministrations of the doctor must end with his patient's death? What follows is "The Light-house" by Edgar Allan Poe. I offer it in homage to the dead poet. May it lay to rest his ghost. Let the reader divine at what place in the story the master laid down his pen and where I, in all humility, took it into my own hand.

▼   ▼   ▼

I am one of the damned. Not as others of my race do I wander the earth in futile search of rest. Nor do I twist under the lash of physical torment. No, mine is a sickness of the soul such as to alienate me from my fellow man, to set me apart from all others without hope of love or friendship.

It was as a boy of ten that I first began to exhibit the strange behavior that has persisted over these thirteen years. Until that time, I had led a life of privilege and luxury, as the third son of the Lord of Friesling. I was unacquainted with affliction or grief.

The day was the Sabbath. I had been seated in the ducal chamber among the young courtiers and nobles who composed the household when a sudden uncontrollable urge to shout came over me. To the horror of those assembled, I interrupted the priestly service with a hoarse guttural cry that had no similarity to the voice of a young boy but was more that of an animal snarling. This was followed by another cry, and another. At my father's order, I was led from the premises in disgrace, beaten, and confined to my rooms. It was the first of many such punishments, none of which had the least effect in putting an end to these outrages. Within weeks, I had added to my repertoire peals of hellish laughter and screams of invective that included the most obscene words in the language, words that a boy of so tender an age would not have been thought to know, words that I must evacuate from my mouth or strangle on them. Even now, I shrink to write them down lest the mere ink upon the page be an invocation to the Devil.

Nor did I select my audience but, to the shame and horror of my next of kin and the entire household, gave forth in front of whatever company happened to be present, plucking from my throat the whole orchestra of curses that were my sole means of relief, however transitory. From this beginning, I advanced to the further extravagance of mimicking my elders, repeating again and again, so as seeming to mock them, whatever phrases they spoke. Before long these utterances were accompanied by a violent thrusting of my tongue, spasms of my head and shoulders, all punctuated by the most disgusting barks, grunts, and hisses. The more punishment I received, the more frequent came the seizures until they occurred as often as ten and fifteen times in the course of a day. My parents and brothers, the servants, too, were distraught. The entire atmosphere of the castle turned to one of despair and gloom. What was to be done with me? At last, I was sent, along with an elderly valet, Nils, to live in an isolated hunting lodge on the edge of a great woods in the far corner of my father's estate. Here, under the aegis of a kindly uncle, I was to live out my dishonored life until such time as I had been reformed.

To this lodge each day, a new physician came *en retinue*, each with his own diagnosis and prescription: blood-letting, purgatives, enemas—all the ghastly therapy of subtraction. When these failed, I was plunged alternately into hot and cold baths; stoups, poultices, and plasters of hot oil and turpentine were applied to my entire body. Bees were placed upon my lips so as to swell them shut with stinging. Emetics and all sorts of obnoxious medications were funneled into my mouth. At length a company of soldiers was dispatched to obtain a flagon of salutary water from the fountain of Saint Hildegard, said to be effective against lycanthropy. A single mouthful of the fetid ammoniacal slime produced the most violent retching and abdominal pain. When these medical martyrdoms produced no subsidence of my horrid idiosyncrasies, I was referred to the priests. What was needed was a thorough exorcism, it was decided. On the appointed day, a Goliath of a priest—he could have strangled a wolf with his rosary—advanced upon me, holding aloft a silver crucifix, grinding his teeth, blowing out his cheeks, sweating until it seemed he, not I, harbored the demon. But when a day and a night of holy gymnastics only incited me to yet greater heights of echolalia, the brutish priest struck the Devil a last righteous blow across the face that left me senseless, and departed.

It was decided that I was mad. But, alas, I was not mad. Nor am I now. Possessed? Infested? Perhaps, but utterly sane. And beyond the power of any mere priest or physician to set me free. Subsisting as it does upon the unnatural violation of the laws of man and God, mine is a perversion of such cunning and tenacity as to confound all but the one whose body is its instrument. I grew familiar with the spiteful characteristics which insisted that the outbursts occur only in the presence of another human being. Alone and out of earshot, I remained beautifully silent. Nor, as the old valet told me, did the eruptions occur in sleep. In my isolated dwelling, with only the necessary presence of Nils and the daily visit of my dear uncle, the demon—for that is what I must call it—lay largely dormant, allowing me some dignity. Yet I was far from happy. My perpetual solitude seems to me a living death. I longed for the comrades I knew I could never have. All day I studied and played like a wild thing, to tire myself out.

Upon my eighteenth birthday, the tenth of February, my uncle presented me with a pair of ornate pistols. Toward midnight, faithful Nils departed after seeing to my needs, but not before I had again scourged him with my tongue, though surely not with my heart, for I had come to love the old man. Yet I disclosed nothing to him of the grim purpose that had suddenly revealed itself to me. Alone, I took up one of the pistols. Through the casement, a full moon washed the contents of my room, where, by the bed, I knelt to pray for forgiveness. Youth bids farewell to the moon more easily than to the sun. But prayer would not come, only a last curse that I flung straight in the face of the cruel God who had created such an aberrance as I. No sooner had it been uttered than the door was flung open and my servant pulled me from the room. The house was in flames, and by daybreak, the lodge and with it my beloved uncle had been consumed. The grief that followed was tainted. I mourned, but in my secret heart I could not but feel that my last terrible oath had called down this conflagration. And not even Death would receive me.

When my brothers arrived, I gave myself into their hands. They brought me back to the ancestral house, where once again I was assailed by the numbers and witch words that called forth the demon. Time and again, family and guests were struck to horrified silence when I spat and brayed and barked. At last I was sequestered in an apartment in a far turret of the castle, attended by the old valet who had saved my wretched life. For companions, I had only my dog, Neptune, and the ancient books that lined the shelves of these rooms. One night, unable to sleep, I chose a volume at random and sat down to read. It was a fatal selection. The book was entitled *The Light-houses of Norland*, one of a set of identically bound volumes that comprised a learned treatise on the history and architecture of these structures. From my first glimpse of the etchings and diagrams with which the texts were illustrated, I was drawn to the stark beauty of the lonely towers, to their utter isolation, and to the benevolence of their purpose. For the next months, I studied these volumes night and day. The final volume was a manual of instruction in the daily tasks and responsibilities of the keeper of a certain light-house called Otterhölm. It was a tome of encyclopedic proportions, written in a weighty Old Testament prose that treated the least likely circumstance *ad infinitum*. Nevertheless, I read it slowly, a page at a time, as if it were the Book of Ecclesiastes. By summer's end I had committed the entire volume to memory.

I was particularly struck by the last page of the manual, which was entitled "In Extremis." It so instructed that in the event that the integrity of the light-house was violated, either by an inrush of sea through a break in the pediment or in the occasion of a fire, the keeper was duty-bound to ensure as well as possible the preservation of the written log in order that the course of events be made known to the Consistory. The keeper was to immerse the entire manuscript in melted candle wax until it was completely sealed, then cast it into the sea, where it might float to safety. The keeper was then to retreat to the lowermost story of the structure, there to await rescue or an honorable death in the line of duty.

In the course of my studies I learned that the light-house of Otterhölm was situated on a reef in midsea that lay no more than a week's voyage from the coast of my father's land. By correspondence with De Grät, the overseer of the realm, I learned further that the beacon of Otterhölm had not been lighted for three years, the keeper having disappeared under certain circumstances and no one found willing to take his place. Since that time, four ships had foundered upon the reef, with much loss of life. All at once my destiny was revealed to me. I would go to Otterhölm as its keeper, there to place my damnation in the service of others. In such worthy solitude I should be rid, if not of the demon, at least of the humiliation that defined my existence on earth.

I made my request at once to DeGrät, and he in turn proposed my appointment to the Consistory. To my surprise, there were difficulties, especially with regard to my refusal of an assistant. The strange fate of my predecessor was mentioned, though I found nothing strange about it. Doubtless the old man, having fallen ill or sustained an injury, and sensing that the end was near, had managed to lash himself to the railing of the upper gallery, where, weeks later, his corpse had been found by the sailors sent to investigate, hideously mangled as if by the feasting of seabirds. The objections of my father had also to be overcome. Would I, he wondered, be able to bear the eternal solitude? Sooner or later it would undermine my sanity, cause me to despair. Nonsense! It was solitude that I sought, solitude that I required. As for companionship, there would be Neptune. In the end, pressure was brought to bear upon several members of the Consistory who were vulnerable; the commission was granted.

▼   ▼   ▼

It is said that at the moment of departure, turning to gaze upon his homeland for the last time, the exile's eyes blaze at the sight of a beloved cup, a pipe stand, the fiddle of his boyhood—some dear object of remembrance. Not mine. The door I closed, closed upon the artifacts of a life not worth living, not one of which I brought away to dote upon.

Before me, the sea was breathing easily as if in sleep, with scarcely a wrinkle in the open water. "It shall not last," the captain muttered into his beard. Throughout that first night the helmsman kept the cutter's prow in the silver lunaqua. We seemed to be riding in a furrow of the moon. But toward morning, a sudden squall arose, a squall made half of sea, half of sky, such that the sails had to be reefed and the direct course abandoned for a more circuitous route. Five nights and days passed before I had my first glimpse of the light-house. Otterhölm! The very name evoked a museum of polished bones. I seemed to hear their exotic clatter above the up-roar of the sea. What a great dark frown of a tower it was, without a sign of hopefulness such as one sees in the upreaching spire of a cathedral. Otterhölm reached for nothing, and at the sight, it was borne home to me how completely I should be thrown back upon myself.

Closer still, the reef came into view, a menacing populace of rocks washed by the sea, now visible, now submerged, as the cutter wallowed and staggered through trough after trough of water and spray. What had seemed from afar smooth rock revealed itself to be fissured and rusticated, and carved into fantastic shapes. Here and there were inscrutable hieroglyphs and the rotten, brine-soaked timbers of old shipwrecks. The light-house had been built upon a flat table of rock on the far end of the reef. From my studies, I knew that to provide a foundation, rocks had been scooped from the sea and heaped into a great pile. Atop this was built a platform of masonry, and all about it a seawall. The only approach to the pediment was by longboat through a narrow passage and into a kind of gully or cove. Here the sea was abnormally convulsed, as the multitude of waves crowded at the top like sheep at a pasture gate.

With the cutter anchored and its sails furled, the first longboat was lowered into the ill-tempered sea. Supported by two of the crew, I was lifted from the hold of the cutter and swung into the small vessel, and Neptune put down beside me. Here it was all noise, with the booming of the waves and the slaver of the sea mouthing the rock. The oarsmen strove mightily to coordinate our passage through the aperture in the rocks with the inrush of a wave. The slightest miscalculation would have us fractured upon the jagged reef. Overhead, a variety of seabirds—redshanks, oystercatchers, herring gulls—shared my terror. The stones all about were smeared with their guano. We entered safely, and in the gully, the sea was calmer. The longboat was drawn alongside a seawall, from which stone steps ascended to the portal. Once again, I was lifted bodily from the boat to the pediment. I had arrived.

Neptune and the supplies having been unloaded, the captain prepared to return to the cutter. To my shame everlasting, I offered my thanks to these good seamen, not with a clasping of hands but with yet another eruption of curses. I could not doubt their satisfaction at having deposited so vile a creature in the middle of the ocean and left him to his own devices. Turning, I entered the tower that was to become my nest, my den, my cocoon. Asylum! I was like a child who has located that hidden corner of the world where he will live with his imaginary companions. Yet even at that first moment there was something sentient about the light-house, an aloofness that did not entirely welcome my intrusion.

1 January 1796

This day—my first in the light-house—I make this entry in my diary, as agreed upon with DeGrät. As regularly as I can keep the journal, I will. But there is no telling what may happen to a man all alone as I am. I may get sick, or worse . . . So far well. The longboat had a narrow escape through the aperture in the reef, but why dwell on that, since I am here, all safe? With the seizures abated and my demon again in hibernation, my spirits are beginning to revive already.

The floor of the first story is some twenty feet above sea level, of heavy oak beams. A trapdoor of the same wood leads down into a submarine extension of the shaft that tomorrow I shall explore. Carved into the masonry is a curving stone staircase that leads to the story above, and from thence to each successive story and to the lantern at the top. It is comprised of 180 steps. My first act was to climb to the lantern itself, to step out upon the circular railed gallery that is open to the elements, from which I looked down over the vast expanse of sea that merges with the sky into a single firmament. There, with Neptune at my side, I felt for all the world like Noah on the deck of the Ark, watching the Flood recede. To be in such a light-house is to be aboard a ship that is forever becalmed. No matter the flogging of the wind, it is the very principle of immobility, yet with the sweet illusion of sailing. It is a kingdom measured out in altitude, with a winding staircase for its only road.

The lamp room is a dome made entirely of prisms of glass so as to magnify the light of the beacon. The lantern itself is a great basin of stone with iron fittings. In accordance with the manual of instruction, I filled the basin with oil and fired the wick. Instantly the dome was transformed into a crucible of brightness and heat. The light-house of Otterhölm had returned to life. Once again I stepped out upon the circular gallery and felt the light-house shudder like the deck of a ship trod by its beloved captain.

Immediately below the lantern are the living quarters. These consist of three rooms, the central and largest being a kitchen, on one wall of which is a great hearth. Here there are cupboards, a large table, and two chairs. The masonry walls are fitted out with dark panels of wood, between which are set sconces. A many-tongued candelabrum sits upon the table. The sole ornament is a coat of arms set upon the wall. This consists of the Cross of Saint

George with four galleons, one in each quarter, and above, a crowned lion holding a scroll with the motto *trinitas in unitate.* The rooms to each side are simply furnished, each with a bed, chair, and armoire. The two stories beneath are used for storage of oil, wood, and other supplies. At each level, the walls of the light-house are pierced by narrow vertical windows, one of which opens off the kitchen onto an enclosed bay. This will serve as a roost for the carrier pigeons, which, save for the infrequent arrival of the cutter, are to be my sole means of communication with the mainland. It is evening and I am writing at the table in the great kitchen. From far below comes the muffled respiration of the sea. With a fire burning in the grate and the faint redolence of sail-cloth and old leather, this room has the intimacy of a ship's cabin.

2 January
Morning. The cutter has a rough passage home, I am sure. But now the sea is again calm. In the distance it lies burnished, like the shield of Achilles. Directly below, the light-house wears a perpetual collar of foam.

5 January
Only four days arrived, and already I am as cozy as an egg in its shell. My duties are surprisingly light. In addition to the tending of the lamp, I am twice daily to make a round of the tower, inspecting it for any disrepair. The solidity of the structure argues against any such dilapidation, as the walls are four feet in thickness and made of blocks of stone, subtly carved so as to dovetail the one into the other. The light-house had been standing for a century already, a triumph of masonry over wind and water.

14 January
How good the sea air may be, only those know who have left the intolerable behind. My affection for Otterhölm grows with each gliding fugitive day of winter. I wake each morning to the

soothing artillery of the sea, the knife-like shrieks of the gulls, the thump of Neptune's tail on the floor, and I am at peace. From the gallery, a liturgical light presides over the forces of nature. I have the sense of eternity being filtered through the vast space and I feel as if my spirit is being cleansed as well. Only now and then, in response to some humanlike sound of sea or bird, does the old disquiet stir.

It is time to speak of the Well. I call it that for want of any rational explanation of its presence. Nowhere except in the manual of instruction did I encounter mention of such a submarine extension of a light-house shaft, and there only the repeated instruction—almost a warning—that the trapdoor be kept shut and bolted at all times, save during the weekly inspection of the lower chamber for any cracks that must be caulked. Despite the thickness of the structure's walls, surely this hollowness of its base must make it more vulnerable to the crushing weight of the sea.

It required all of my strength to raise the hatch of the trapdoor. From its depths emanated a cold, sour belch of air. Wooden steps lead down to a ledge that encircles the cavern. A wooden bridge traverses the pool, above which hang strands of mist. Into its depth, by an ingenious tracery of grooves and pipes, is led the rainwater to be used for drinking and bathing. Holding aloft a torch, I descended the steps into what seemed the dark wet gullet of the light-house. In the damp saturated air the torch burned low, struggling to stay alive. Here the climate is humid and breathing difficult. A pale, greenish gleam arises from the sweating walls, where small plants have taken root in the interstices of the masonry blocks. These are further speckled with patches of lichen. In the subdued light of the torch, strange shadows on the walls break apart, collide, fuse, chase one another in a wild metamorphosis. With each step downward, the darkness thickens, the heaviness of the air presses down upon the intruder. I saw that the walls are not vertical here but form an ever-narrowing cone into which the rainwater collects. And it is silent, for one no longer hears the buffeting of the sea, only feels its immense, silent weight. What could have possessed the builders of this light-house to place at its core this *cisterna magna*, like the lowest circle of Dante's *Inferno*, where Satan weeps "with six eyes"?

In the midst of my exploration, a violent tremor seized me, a dread that was less physical than a terror of the soul. I took the steps as quickly as I dared, lowered the hatch, and ascended to the safety of my room. Even here I shudder at the charge of malignant energy that shot through the compartment beneath the sea.

I have resolved to descend to the Well only to perform the weekly inspection prescribed by the manual. Fortunately, there is a rope by which water may be brought up in a bucket through the hatch.

20 January
One day into the next without event. Here the simplest laws of life impose their ritual, encouraging a discipline the soul welcomes after a lifetime of chaos. The light-house has become for me a microcosm of the earth itself, in which I am to dwell between the Lamp above and the Well below, precisely as between Heaven and Hell. In the simplicity and regularity of my duties, a certain languor has invaded the light-house. If I miss anything from my former life, it is the forest—the crackling of leaves underfoot, the unexpected fall of a dead branch, rain dripping leaf to leaf—but such longings have grown less and less frequent. I should count my contentment complete, save that, now and then, the immensity of my solitude sits like a dark beast upon my chest.

I said I should not visit the Well until I must. But I had not counted on its mysterious attraction. Resolve as I will to avoid it, time and again my thoughts are drawn there until I must return to peer from the ledge at my own hideously distorted reflection. What a deceitful, perfidious liquid that presents itself in the bucket in repose, limpid, with "beaded bubbles winking at the brim." Under no circumstances can I persuade Neptune to accompany me. No sooner do I raise the trapdoor than the poor creature begins to whimper and will not cease until I have emerged and the hatch is again lowered.

1 February

I do not know what it was that caused me to awaken just at dawn with the feeling that something untoward had transpired. I only half remembered a dull grinding noise in my sleep, as of something breaking apart. All day yesterday and far into the night a storm had raged. Looking out, I saw that sea and sky were sealed in a bluish mineral light. I climbed to the dome to find that during the night the lantern had gone out! Caught up in the strange reverie brought on by the storm, I had drifted into sleep without seeing to the fire. I had let my duties lapse. Quickly, I poured oil into the basin of the lamp and relit the fire, then stepped out upon the gallery. Through a spyglass I saw, wedged upon the reef some thousand yards from the light-house, a three-master, her sheets doubly reefed. Her prow was splintered, and the sea poured in and out of the hull. With each salvo of waves, she shuddered, turned as on a pivot, and dipped to lie further on her side like a horse held down for branding. There was no sign of her crew, save, some distance from the wreck, a lone figure lying motionless upon the rocks, his tiny form washed over by the sea. I hastened down the steps and out the doorway, down the rocks to the gully, where the dory was moored. I pulled toward the opening in the rocks, then waited and waited until a receding wave should sweep me through the narrows into the open sea. All about me the pitiless reef bared its teeth. Was it guilt at my dereliction that drove me on? Or the immense burden of my solitude that craved human companionship? How I pulled on the oars, for hours it seemed, until I came to the rocks where shuddered the poor wreck. Through the staved hull I saw the bodies of two men, their faces already studded with crabs. Then out upon the black shoulder of the reef I climbed to kneel by the rock pool all laced with ice where lay the dashed and broken body of the man. I stopped only long enough to determine that life, however faintly, yet stirred in him, then lifted him, limp as the dead, and placed him in the dory. I doubted my strength for the return. But for once, Heaven was looking over my shoulder. At the opening to the gully I waited to receive the carrying wave, surrendered to it, and found myself alongside the pediment. Securing the dory, I carried the man to the room opposite mine, where he now lies—breathing, yes, but little more than that. I stripped off the clothing and saw a great gash in the left breast with a fragment of rib sticking through, and another wound to the thigh. His left arm hangs like a flail. His color is that of the waves, and his respiration the labored gurgling of the moribund. I doubt he will survive.

How I cursed my fatal lassitude that brought about this tragic circumstance. Gazing down at the broken body of the stranger, I felt the sudden unbearable weight of my loneliness. What I wished with all my heart was to know the companionship of the fellow being. In the wild excitement of the moment, I had forgotten that it is only in absolute solitude that I can live without the torment of my affliction. It was my desperate hope to retrieve that man, to retrieve him for myself.

11 February

For ten nights the northern sky has been hung with the curtains of a sickbed. For ten days and nights the sailor has lain insensible, as though his heart could not decide at what moment to cease beating. He has uttered not a sound, except for the clicks, gasps, and sucking noises that accompany his breathing. Again and again, I give thanks for the chest of salves and medicaments thrust upon me by old Nils on my departure. With these herbal decoctions and unguents, I have been able to dress the sailor's wounds, although with scant hope for his life. Yet once, in his delirium, he reached out a hand, which I took between my own and held it as if to say to the feverish man, *I am here*. At once he calmed, and a moment later sank into a peaceful sleep.

16 February

This morning I entered the room to see that the sailor's eyes were open, and that when I moved, his gaze followed me. I bent over him to speak.

"You are alive," I told him. It seemed necessary to persuade him of that. And I related briefly the story of the shipwreck and his rescue. He made not the least reply, but gaped blankly as if stunned. I drew a chair to the bed and questioned him as to his name, his past, the points of departure and destination of the wrecked vessel. Still he made no reply. I attributed his silence to the state of shock brought on by his terrible ordeal.

Nor have I yet heard a sound emerge from his lips other than the grunts and hiccups of a man in delirium. The wretchedness of his physical state touches me deeply. The least movement causes him to grimace, his breathing to grow shallow and rapid. Yet still he makes no outcry. It is a rare stoicism.

19 February

It is three days since the sailor has regained his consciousness. He has begun to accept gruel, which I feed him with a wooden spoon. Now and then he lifts his gaze to mine, then lowers his eyes as if to silence what they would tell. Again I questioned him gently about his native land, his name, but he seems to have lost all knowledge of the past and, with seeming lack of understanding, answers neither yea or nay. I offered him pen and paper to write down what he would not speak. By a shake of his head he gave me to understand that he cannot read or write.

1 March

Today I gathered sea-gull eggs from the nests inside the seawall. I had to smile to see the eagerness with which my patient took the omelet I made from them. His strength improves by the day. The pallor of near-death has been replaced by a whiteness of skin that is startling—as though, by himself, he constitutes a new race. Who could his people be?

I sit at the table writing in the ledger while outside the gulls circulate like smoke. Otterhölm is roofed by a low sky. Seals are crying on the reef with the voices of the drowned. In the next room the mariner sleeps.

12 March
Each day the man grows stronger, eating whatever I place before him. Now and then he looks up at me with the dumb, submissive expression of a beast. I confess to a certain pride in having salvaged this man from the wreck. And yet, with his recovery, something is stirring within me. It is, I know, the demon, who senses the presence of another human being. Day by day the pressure is mounting. Already when I am with him the struggle to contain myself is acute. He must leave by the next cutter. I cannot risk his presence here.

12 April
In Mathias, for that is what I have named him, I recognize a kindred taste for solitude, and a certain nostalgia, as though he exists at some distance from the world. Yet he is no stranger to industry. In what passes for carpentry here he has made traps with which to catch crayfish. And from a plan he has fashioned a fine harpoon. With it, only yesterday he slew a seal that had ventured too close to the seawall. We shall have fresh meat instead of the wormy hardtack to which we are accustomed. At tending the lamp he is utterly dependable. His mariner's soul is visible in the way he gazes at sea and sky, as if to make an offering of himself. He seems to sense long beforehand the coming of a storm, all the mysteries of the tides, the vagaries of the inconstant sea. Twice, when the sea was calm, we rowed to the site of the shipwreck and

returned with a load of wood from the hull to supplement our supply. Though he does not speak, there are times when I seem to hear the murmuring of his flesh. Does he place his trust in silence as in the whirlwind? Only one proscription has he placed upon himself: He visits every portion of the reef and every story of the tower, except the Well. That, I see, is to be my precinct.

24 April
By the pantomime we have invented, I have made known to Mathias my intention that he leave the light-house on the next ship. Was it only fancy that I saw upon his face a look of sadness at the news?

2 May
It has happened as I knew it would. I was at my writing table. There, where the floor rises two steps to the embrasure of the kitchen window, Mathias stood gazing out. All at once I felt mounting the terrible urge that will not be defined, felt the hot ball of rage rising in my throat. I bit my lips until the blood ran on my chin. I clamped my very soul shut about the demon. I leaped to my feet, overturning the chair, and covered my face with upflung arms. But in the end, it was no use. The dam burst in my throat, I heard the harsh grating noises, the hideous gargles, curses, all the filth of my speech. On and on I spewed until the rage was spent. In the silence that followed, Mathias gave no sign that he had heard me. When at last he turned and stepped down from the window, I saw only the perfect innocence of his expression. Then it was that I knew the truth. He had not heard. The one human being whom Fate had sent to share my isolation was the only one with whom I could live. Mathias is deaf. His muteness is the silence of the deaf man who has never learned to speak. With that knowledge, a wave of relief, not to say happiness, came over me. And I felt the thwarted demon shrink back into hibernation.

24 June

The cutter has come. Through the glass I watched its approach not with any sense of anticipation, but with mounting dread. Together, from the gallery, Mathias and I watched its perilous approach to the opening of the gully, the letting down of the small boats loaded with provisions. And with each succeeding step in the unloading, my heart grew heavier. I did not want him to go. At the end, I accompanied him to the seawall, from which he was to step into the boat. At the last moment, he turned to me with an imploring look and, I thought, tears in his eyes. I could not be strong. We bade farewell to the men and watched them pole off. The boat rejoined its ship, the anchor was raised, and a blessed length of empty sea appeared between ship and light-house. Together, Mathias and I reentered our tower.

18 August

One day into the other in which Mathias and I carry out our daily round. Side by side, we work in the silence that has been imposed upon us, the silence that is my blessing and, doubtless, his curse. In the absence of speech, I listen to the sounds he makes: the faint strokes of his oars, the scrape of his boot on the floor, something like a hiss when he stoops to retrieve the fresh-caught cod from the dory. In such quietude, a sneeze or a cough is an oration. And welcome. No more perfect a partner in exile could have been conceived. His small acts of solicitude in the tending of the fire, the preparation of food, the operation of the lantern, he performs without the least show of servitude, but with a kind of dignity. He is at once robust and delicate, a man snugly lodged in his body, and with a pulse that I imagine to be slower than that of other men, as though the fire of his life has been banked. Or is it a pensiveness natural to the deaf, who are said to be gifted with special insight? When we pass each other on the steps, it is as though he is awakening from a dream while I am falling into it. At the moment when we stand together, we become one.

15 September
Word has come from DeGrät by pigeon that the mainland has been swept by a plague. Nor has the noble household been spared. My two brothers have been stricken to death, and I, demonized and isolate, am sole heir. But I should far rather be keeper of this light-house than lord of a realm. Strangely, I am unable to feel the grief natural to a man whose family and homeland have been laid waste, as though the sentiments of patriotism and kinship were of a former life from which I long ago departed into a new incarnation.

19 September
This morning, in accordance with the instructions in the manual, I went to carry out the weekly inspection of the Well. Mathias had left the light-house to gather in crayfish from the traps he had sunk about the reef. No sooner had I raised the hatch of the trapdoor, than I felt once again the presence of evil inherent in that low compartment. The sense of oppression was greater than before, as though whatever presence dwelt therein had swelled, and the very air seemed to have grown viscous, weighting my arms and legs. I made my way along the ledge about the pool, clinging to the whimpers of Neptune above as to a life-line in a wild sea. Halfway around, the torch blazed up, then died, but not before I had glimpsed a pale, shapeless mass submerged in the dark pool just below where I stood. A moment later, it rolled like a corpse and sank from view with a swarming of eddies. The depth swallowed my strength as if I were a stone cast into it. In the utter blackness I clung to the rail and forced myself to continue toward the opening of the trapdoor. At last I achieved the steps and climbed out to lie panting on the floor. When I had recovered somewhat, I lowered the hatch and, without daring to look back, ascended to my room. There I sat, trembling and unable to steady my pen, the stench of the Well in my nostrils, its damp upon my skin. Suddenly, my dread lifted, and I

looked up to see that Mathias had entered the room, bringing with him that special silence which always causes me to hold my breath for fear of shattering it. The very look upon his face restored my composure. Perhaps I had imagined the apparition in the Well? Perhaps it was a hallucination, an odd trick of light and shadow, a configuration brought about by the shimmering of the pool?

12 October

The cutter has arrived but there is too much sea in the gully for the longboat to pass through. And so she must lie to. I have decided not to present myself at the unloading to spare the innocent seamen my unwarranted abuses. Mathias will receive them.

13 October

The sea calmed sufficiently for the provisions to be unloaded. Mathias made several trips to the cutter in the longboat. Excellent mariner that he is, familiar with every rocky projection and current of the reef, his guidance proved indispensable. Or so I judged, watching from the gallery. When the longboat had departed for the last time, I descended to find him holding a kitten in his arms. Unaware of my presence, he stroked and kissed the creature, his face suffused with tenderness. So there are to be four of us.

15 October

Toward the newcomer Neptune has shown all the generosity of spirit of which a dog is capable, insisting only upon his sovereignty at the foot of my bed. Mathias keeps the kitten with him. At dawn to-day, on my way to the lantern, I glanced through the doorway to see the little cat creep from his sleep-tangled arms. I am awed by its domesticating power. By the addition of this one, we are made a family.

30 October

Word by carrier pigeon from DeGrät that we can no longer
rely on the cutter for supplies, the mariners having been deci-
mated by the plague. By trimming the lantern during daylight, I
have calculated that there is sufficient lamp oil to last another
three months. Surely by then we shall be resupplied. As for food
and fuel for ourselves, we have no such anxiety. There is the
immense fecundity of the sea and its reefs and the ingenuity of
Mathias.

When the waters are quiet, he can be seen crouching on the
wall over the gully, spear upraised. More often than not, there is
fish for our supper. Wood from the shipwreck is ours for the taking, although it still grieves me to think that our warmth depends
upon the drowned.

Mathias has no fear of the water. This morning he stood on the
seawall, stripped, and leaped into the sea. Moments later, there he
was again, glistening like a seal on the rocks. To me, the waves
are so many blows in the face. It is a flagellation from which I
emerge stinging and red and cold.

We live under the one authority of the lamp, which transforms
our every task into a ritual of worship. Pouring oil into the basin
of the lantern from an earthenware jug that he tips from his
shoulder, Mathias seems to me like some biblical priest preparing
the altar, his face in the uprush of flame the gleaming visage of an
angel. Feeding the fire, polishing the dome, he and I are companions in a dream, two children creating the night. Later, we sit
together at the table, he working a piece of driftwood with his
knife, I writing in this journal while the logs in the grate glow and
dim, glow and dim, as if in rhythm with the wind that howls
about the tower.

Yet there is something about his silence that, argue as I will
against it, disturbs me. At moments I doubt the very perfection of
it, and wonder whether it is true deafness or some other form of
hearing. Perhaps, displaced from his ears, the sense has taken up

residence elsewhere in his body. There is a voice, too, I swear it, that rises about him, issuing from his very flesh. It is then that I feel, however faintly, something angry stirring in my soul, something altogether familiar. I must arrest these perverse thoughts.

15 November

Still Mathias's silence torments me. More and more I suspect not true deafness but a refusal to speak that has the quality of a dangerous concealment. This morning, sitting behind him in the dory, I leaned forward and gave a mighty shout. Was it coincidence that made him turn at that instant with a watchful look that vanished almost before I caught it? Why should he deceive me, who rescued him?

20 November

The past weeks have been full of toil. In addition to our routine we have undertaken to clean and polish the light-house as though it were a ship. Mathias has accepted the wearying pace I have imposed upon us without the least sign of resentment, while I, in a frenzy of activity, hope like the monk who doubles his prayers to stifle what threatens to defile me from within.

With suspicion, the light-house itself has become a tower of shadows that each day grows more tenebrous. No longer is Otterhölm my haven of solitude, my refuge. But still it may be my university,where I shall learn the truth.

I have become a secret watcher, a spy. Oh, this distrust that breeds itself anew each day and which alone is capable of calling up the creature who lusts to be heard! For some days I have felt the premonitory aura. Daily the pressure mounts. How is it that I only now perceive a certain subtlety about him?

22 November

Again! We had just finished our evening meal. I had seated myself at the table to begin to write. Mathias was tending the grate. All at once, I felt the involuntary movements of my mouth, the baring and crunching of my teeth, the bursting apart of my throat. Then out came the curses, black as ravens, flapping and cawing from my mouth. The ill-said words disgorged, my lips torn as if by the passage of thorns, I watched him turn toward me, saw his face redden as if slapped. He hears! I know it! Or was it a glow from the flames over which he bent? I will conquer these insane suspicions or I will go mad.

24 November

At noon I opened the trapdoor to haul up fresh water from the Well only to find that the rope had broken. It would be necessary to descend to retrieve the bucket. For a long time I held the frayed end of the rope, fingering the groove in the stone where it had ridden. At last I descended to the Well, upon whose scabbed and oozing walls the torch cast veins of light. Once again, from the footbridge, I beheld the creature stalking me from beneath the surface of the black liquid element in which it lives and which is surely not water but something like blood. By a will other than my own, my gaze was held fast to what now appeared as a loose, voluptuous bag, whose undifferentiated contents flowed from one part to another, causing the whole to ripple in languorous sacculations and invaginations, as though the beast were taking sensual pleasure in itself. No chimera of the brain this, but an amphibian reality perceived through the unconscious reflexes of the spinal cord—boneless, bloodless, fleshless, composed of some primordial jelly that existed at the beginning of life. Upon what does it feed if not in its own miasma that has the odor of gangrene? Even as I watched, the creature grew turgid, polypoid, like something possessed of a fierce embryonic energy and undergoing metamorphosis, evolving toward a yet more evil incarnation. And I knew beyond any doubt that *here* is manufactured the dark concentrate of evil itself, which emanates to spread across the earth and pass into the bodies of men, there ceaselessly to excite the inmost self in gross circumvention of natural law. At last I tore myself from the hypnotic pool and fled up to my room to lie trembling upon the bed. At length, exhaustion overcame me and I slept.

Hours later, I awoke with the odor of gangrene still strong in my nostrils. With a start I recollected that in my haste and terror, *I had not shut the trapdoor.* At the black mouth of the hatchway, I found poor Neptune, stiff, already cold, his bloody muzzle overhanging the edge.

4 December
I know now that whatever dwells beneath Otterhölm is gathering itself, the way darkness thickens to form night. All day I prowl the light-house, a trespasser fearing discovery. I press my ear to the walls, to the trapdoor even, but this evil makes no sound that I can hear. Only its smell grows stronger, clinging to me like smoke. At night I am awakened by cold fingers of mucus in my throat. As if in conspiracy with the creature, the man Mathias continues his daily round, only now he makes as if to hide as I pass. Is he a man? Or only something pretending to be one? Oh, this expectancy is unbearable. If it will come, let it come now.

20 December
The equinoctial gales have begun. I awoke to a sky of steel-blue tones that darkened by the hour to purple, then black, as the storm gathered. Archipelagoes of clouds advanced upon the lighthouse. Just before nightfall, broke such a storm as I have not seen in my tenure at Otterhölm. Within minutes the sea was a creature in estrus, bellowing for its mate; above it raged a wind that could strip flesh from bone. So vast an expanse of liquid in motion cannot but awaken an antique terror, yet tinged with the strange pleasure one feels when snugly enclosed in its midst. Now and then the tower shudders as a great boulder wrenched from the depths crashes against the pediment. Up and down the steps

Mathias and I climb like sleepwalkers. To comfort the frightened little cat, he has placed it inside his shirt. Amid the thunder claps, his own face is a blank page, except—but no, I tell myself, it was an apocalyptic streak of lightning that caused him once to flinch, stiffen. Still, more than ever, he eyes me a thousand times with a single look.

The Next Day

In the midst of the tempest, Mathias came to inform me that the lantern had gone out. Together we climbed to the dome, each with a pail of oil. Mathias held the torch. As soon as it was lit, I hurried to fetch another pail of oil, and another. Thus we toiled in the brightness and heat until the cistern was full and the beacon once again in full blaze. To escape the heat of the dome Mathias stepped out upon the gallery. From within, I watched him leaning on the railing as if it were the deck of a foundering ship, his eyes neither opened nor closed, but like those of a marble head; his lip parted as if to *speak*! Through the refracting prismatic dome he was transfigured, with wings of fire rising from his shoulders and all about him a brilliance that rendered him translucent.

What followed took place as if in a dream. I recall only the sudden epilepsy of rage, the lurching of my body from the dome to the gallery, the familiar pressure in my throat; how he turned toward me, his face a mask of innocence, how slowly my hands returned to me, balled into fists. I did not see him fall, if fall he did. Only heard a cry, a single pure call like the sound of the last trumpet that rang out for the time it would take a man to plunge to the reef.

▼   ▼   ▼

Shrouded in whiteness, the light-house totters. The next blast will send it crashing. Already the glass dome is shattered, the gallery avulsed from the wall. A great jagged fault has appeared at the base of the tower. With each hour, it extends itself upward with a crackling sound as the masonry splits. In all the light-house there is no living thing but I. I, and that which awaits me in the Well. For the last time I sit at the table in the room where Mathias and I have shared so many silences. From the sconces and from the tongues of the candelabrum, I have taken the tapers. My only light is the flames of the hearth, where the wax melts. In accordance with the instructions in the manual, the journal must be dipped and cooled three times until it is completely encased. When that is done, and this book consigned to the waves, I shall descend the steps of Otterhölm for the last time to rejoin the depravity of which I am no more than an outpost, to stare myself back into it, to have its eyes stare out of mine, to fuse with the unrefusable. There is nothing else left for me, nothing at all. Should this record I have kept only to give pain a name survive to wash upon some distant shore, I pray that the finder be not lettered, for I have come to know the terrible contagion of words, their power to destroy.

IMAGINE A WOMAN

Imagine a woman, youngish, not quite thirty. Her brown hair falls toward her arm as she sits at a small table, writing in a notebook. It is night and the single lamp behind her chair gives a meager light. Now and again, she rises to pace the small room. Then you can see that she is thin, but with the large belly of pregnancy, perhaps six months. When she feels the child move, she winces and presses her hand to her abdomen as though to still it. Once outside the circle of lamplight, she is no more than a concentrate of darkness. Only when she returns to sit can you see that she is pale, with delicate features—not beautiful, but there is a grace in the way she turns her head or moves her hand across the page. Imagine the quick tiny hiss as it slides along the paper an inch at a time, from left to right, then the longer hiss from right to left as she begins a new line.

My dear Hugh,

I confess to an ignoble pleasure as I imagine you holding this package in your hands, turning it over, reading the return address. Who in the world is S. Gallant, you wonder, before taking a scissors to the twine that Madame Durand, in accordance with my precise instructions, will have tied around the wrapping paper. Veyrier, France? But by then you will have recognized the handwriting and torn your way through to the contents. You and I have been here before—do you remember? Ten years ago, when we were driving from Geneva to Avignon, we stopped in Annecy to see the Convent of La Visitation. Afterward, going south along the lake, we passed the Veyrier. I remembered the sign. I even glimpsed this *pension*, the Hotel les Acacias, by the side of the road, midway between the mountain and the lake below, as we drove by. It is just an old farmhouse, really, with a steeply slanted roof and wide overhanging eaves and, in front, a terrace set with tables.

It is one year since I left. This journal, the first words you will have had from me since then, will also be the last. If as I implored you, you have made no attempt to find me, I thank you for that. If you have made such attempts, you see that they were in vain. It is laughably easy to disappear. I will not tell you the details of my zigzag journey, only that a number of borders were violated and more than one palm crossed with silver . . . Oh, dear! All at once my pen has turned stiff and arthritic. How to begin?

Under the circumstances, divorce was absurd. Squander the little time left to me in recriminations and remorse? Staying with you was equally absurd. You see, Hugh, while I do not hate you, neither do I love you. I think now that I never did. They say that in illness one is laid open to revelation. The truth is—don't take offense—I ceased to think about you at all. It is the egotism of the sick, a shortcoming for which I forgive myself with the suspicion that it was never me whom you loved; it was marriage, the idea of it. That having been said, there was this, too: I did not want to die prematurely of a virus; I wanted to have *lived*, for no matter how short a time. I could never do that had I stayed.

▼   ▼   ▼

It was best that I knew first. Had it been you, I wonder whether you could have withstood the anguish of telling me.

"There is something I must tell you," the obstetrician said. Oh, the voice, the face of a man who can bear such tidings. Even before he had finished, a tiny needle of ice had punctured my heart.

"And the child?" I wanted to know.

"There is every likelihood of that too."

I went home with my secret and waited like an assassin until your back was turned before I thrust the words between your shoulder blades. I watched you stiffen, turn, your gaze lashed to mine.

"How do you think it happened?" you said.

"I don't know. And you?"

"No," you said, so quietly. But it was a lie, for there had been Manuel. How easily I write his name, as if he were someone I knew or had seen. I used to try to give him a physical appearance. All I know is that he is a Filipino, and that he is twenty-nine, my age. From these threads I have stitched a slender, short, fine-boned man with black hair and dark complexion. His eyes, too, are dark, with a slight tilt. While I was at it, I gave him even, white teeth and a sweet smile, this stranger come from the other side of the world with his fatal gift of beauty.

▼　▼　▼

From my note you have known everything that, up to now, I have wanted you to know: that I had taken enough money and morphine (again, do not ask) to free myself from anxiety and discomfort, and that I did not hate you. You are hardly to blame for the gray rain of virus that is falling over the earth. Nor do I condemn your secret love. Despite all, I continue to marvel at love however one locates it.

I left to reclaim the life I had surrendered to a convention that kept me from the *real* real—the one that exists just beneath the surface of things. It is what I have come here to find. Already it has begun to happen. I have become strangely receptive to the moon, the waterfall, the trees, the bread, the wine,

all the components of this magic village. As my immunity to the
germs has dwindled, so has my resistance to these "influences."
It is the heightened sensitivity of fever, some might say, or the
clarifying effect of pain.

Do you think that I am bored? Not at all. Boredom is a symp-
tom of civilization and I have become a pagan. It is as though a
fog has blown away and I live in a clear, crystalline air, where
everything has a voice. I am not so naive or sentimental as to
believe that there are spirits in the rocks, forests, and mountains,
spirits that must be placated. It is something else, a property of
the elements itself that is capable of affecting one for better or for
worse. Do you imagine tears falling on the page? Don't. If weeping could coax fate, then perhaps I would weep. But I have given
up all my lamentations. When there is no one to tell your grief to,
it makes sense to stop.

▼   ▼   ▼

Madame Durand, the concierge, appears to be in her seventies.
When she is not trudging up and down the stairs in her felt slip-
pers, Madame sits in a cubbyhole off the front hall knitting or
with her cheek resting on a forefinger, eyes half shut like a sleepy
old tabby cat, but not missing a trick. She has the obligatory dyed
blond hair of the postmenopausal Frenchwoman, which, along
with the bright yellows, reds, and purples she favors, gives her the
look of a clump of mixed tulips. She has a slight limp, the residue
of a hip operation.

You can imagine the state of fatigue and discomfort in which I
arrived. Madame asked me no questions, nor did she show the
least sign of surprise or curiosity that a pregnant woman, wild-
eyed and panting, should appear unannounced at her hotel at ten
o'clock at night. I had the unaccountable feeling that she had
been expecting me. I followed her up the two flights of stairs to
my little room under the eaves. *"Dormez,"* she said with a great

solemnity as she left. And sleep I did, fell into bed like an apple from a tree, and slept until the sun crossed the mountain behind the house and burst into my window. Or was it the baby stirring that woke me?

There are fourteen rooms in the hotel. Mine is at the front, on the third floor in the corner. The stairs are narrow, steep, and dark, but I am not yet so ill that I cannot manage them.

If asked to describe my soul, I would describe this room. Great wooden beams divide the ceiling. The single tall French window has an inner ledge that is wide enough to sit on. Leaning out, with my long hair hanging down, I feel like Rapunzel. At one time, this was a loft where chickens and geese were kept in winter. They roosted in the niche carved in one wall, which is occupied now by a toilet, sink, and mirror. There is a narrow bed with a long cylindrical pillow that I must fold in thirds in order to sleep. It is easier to breathe that way. To write, I sit on this ladder-back chair at a plain table, both of walnut, as is the small armoire. The room was obviously not consulted about the wallpaper which is a neoclassic pattern that I rather like—women in drapery carrying amphorae and lolling about columns, all done in faded ivory and silver. Of all the rooms of my life, this is surely the most congenial.

From my window, I look down over the rooftops of the village to the lake. Directly below is the dining terrace, punctuated by the seven old acacia trees from which the hotel takes its name. A new highway has diverted much of the traffic that used to run in front of the inn. Now only bicycles, horse-drawn carts, and the occasional bus pass by. Most of the time it is quiet, save for the waterfall and the *"hola!"* a farmer calls to his horse.

This morning I told Madame that I would be staying for an indefinite period of time. My accommodation goes by the name *demipension*, under which I do not select from the menu but am to be fed whatever is prepared in the kitchen for the help. It is delightfully inexpensive. Anyway, I do not want to think about food; I do not plan to eat much of it.

As for worldly diversions, I might as well be living in a cloister. The only "life" takes place on the terrace, where, in good weather, meals are served. Even when I can eat nothing, I go to sit there. I wouldn't miss it for the world. There are fifteen tables set under the acacias. The trunks are as big and strong as men, and their foliage is dense enough to shelter us from any but a vigorous downpour. All through dinner we are kept company by a family of saucy sparrows. Only a raised boot heel directly overhead will scatter them, and as soon as the all-clear sounds, they're once again pecking the gravel for tidbits or perched on the back of a chair.

Quiet as it is all day, at dinner the tables on the terrace are filled. Most of the other guests are French and Swiss, many of whom I take to be regulars from the warmth with which Madame and the Portuguese girls greet them. Each table is covered with a starched white cloth. Alongside each plate is a linen envelope embroidered with the number of your room. Mine is number fourteen. The napkin inside it is changed once a week, on Monday. It is expected that each of us, at the end of the meal, will fold the napkin and replace it in the envelope. A beautifully frugal custom. No human being is entitled to a fresh linen napkin every day.

In addition to Madame, there is Philippe, her grandson, a husky *savoyard* of seventeen, with the square head and short-barreled torso of the men of this region. He has lovely big ears that shine when sunlight passes through them, and a yoke of shoulders already powerful. Toward me, he is shy and courteous in equal part. Two pretty, cheerful Portuguese girls, each about twenty, wait on the tables. If there is a restaurant in Heaven, these two will be hired to serve the gods. It is their favorite pastime to tease Philippe, and his calvary to endure it. His suffering takes the form of a tuneless whistling in which he wraps himself. Still, if I were those Portuguese flirts, I would take care. Philippe is almost a man. With every step he deepens his hold on this hotel, which will one day be his. And more than once, I have caught sight of something like phosphorus blazing in his eyes.

Somewhere inside the kitchen, there is a chef—there must be, but no one has ever seen him. Perhaps he is kept on a tether lest he fly off to the Ritz. I can eat only as much as one of the sparrows. More is not urged upon me, thank God. It is a wisdom of the body that anorexia be the proper condition of the fatally ill; one must lighten oneself for the crossing over.

The village is small, no more than two thousand feet long, bracketing the narrow gravel road. At night it has a hallucinated look. Perhaps it is the moonlight that dapples the trees and cottages and is drawn out into a shining filament across the lake. The two silent cows that are left to spend the night in the yard are flecked with it, and the stripe of road goes dark and bright as it ascends. Everything—houses, trees, animals—appears to have surrendered its solidity and to be permeable, wavering, as if at any moment Veyrier itself will turn molten and begin to flow. The only thing here that is dense and corporeal is me; I am like the pit of a peach about which this soft incandescent village has deposited itself.

▼   ▼   ▼

I have not seen a watch or clock in weeks. (You wouldn't survive here for a day.) Now it is the hour of the Angelus, when the bells of La Visitation come visiting me from across the lake. *Bong! Bong! Bong!* In the vast choir of French bells, this one is the baritone. I like to think of that convent full of virgins lying beneath such a deep-chested Don Giovanni, obeying his every summons.

▼   ▼   ▼

A bluish spot has appeared on my arm, the size of a grain of rice. I was told to expect them. Fever, night sweats, shortness of breath. All night I paddled my bed around the room, like a canoe in whitewater. In and out of the alcove swam phosphorescent fish. And the sounds that came from my chest! Like two pieces of dry leather rubbing together, then the click of billiard balls colliding. Toward morning I forced myself to lie still, as though I were already dead and had no need to move, had forgotten how to move. Then sleep came. I awoke to the bells that came across the lake like skipping stones. Aside from the convent bells and the mute presence of a small church opposite the *mairie*, I see no evidence here of "religion." So far as I know, the people do not go to mass; nor have I seen a priest.

▼   ▼   ▼

This morning I arose and went to take a bath; only to find that the tub had been filled, the soap and towels at hand. When I returned to my room, a fire had been laid in the little stove, and bundles of lavender and thyme had been placed in with the kindling. When I touched it with a match, the room filled with the odor of herbs. Within moments, my breathing had calmed. Who is so good to me?

▼   ▼   ▼

Dawn: A mule, his ears still drowsy, pulls a cart noisily down to the market. It is piled so high with logs that it scarcely clears the lower branches of the plane trees.

Noon: A blue heat presses down on the village.

Evening: After dinner I walked down to the village, no more than two hundred paces, but about all I could manage.

I feel as though I have lived here before and have returned after a long journey. Nothing—not a shed or a hedge or a cobblestone or a crooked lamp—strikes me with the least surprise. Rather, for every object I feel a faint, fond sense of recognition. And also I feel the telepathic undercurrent that binds each house to the next, and each inhabitant to the others. I long to tap into it, to become porous.

▼   ▼   ▼

It is April, and the noise of the waterfall drowns out any other sound. Some distance behind the hotel the melting snow plunges down the sheer face of the mountain to form a pool whose runoff surges straight for Les Acacias. Just before we should be swamped, the torrent politely divides into twin channels that course on either side of us and disappear beneath the road on their way to the lake below. We are, as it were, islanded, and after a while, one does not even hear the roar of the water. It is strangely cleansing, and gives me the illusion that I am no longer infected—in the same way, I suppose, that a paraplegic is given back the motion of his limbs when he lies on the deck of a small sailboat. On some damp days I walk as far as the pool at the foot of the waterfall to stand in the mist. You can't go any farther, as beyond that the mountain defends itself with a Maginot Line of briers. As for the lake, Hugh, first imagine the Dead Sea; then conceive of its opposite, and you have this lake of Annecy that lies among the mountains like a boss on Achilles' shield.

▼   ▼   ▼

A half dozen black doctors from Mali have come to the hotel. Four men and two women, all slender and tall, the men in suits and neckties, the women in vivid robes and hats. They had been attending a conference in Geneva. They are exceedingly polite to one another. The knives and forks leap in their long fingers, and they meet my gaze with the most refined nod of greeting. After dinner, the girls sang for them in Portuguese.

▼   ▼   ▼

The doctors of Mali have left, and now the *pension* is full of Swiss. My God, they are hideous—misshapen, tuberous, and gray from a lifetime of having eaten too many potatoes, with gigantic buttocks and only the vaguest impression of a face imprinted on a slab of flesh. I watched one man tearing meat from a bone like a dog gargling beer. At the end, he broke off a piece of bread and cleaned his teeth with it! How different from the slender, mercurial Africans with their flashing eyes and teeth, their spidery fingers. Nor do they have the innate courtesy of the Malinese. They stared at me so, I could only hope that the vestiges of my human form would suffice. Now there's your old Monica—the asp in a basket of fig leaves. I'd better close for today. So much of this journal has been written by moonlight. Can you tell? From the strain of lunacy that runs through it?

▼   ▼   ▼

It is Midsummer Eve. In the mountain villages, huge bonfires have been set. One by one they were lit until the lake was ringed with points of fire. On the terrace, red and yellow paper lanterns have been strung in the acacias. Though it is too early for dinner, I am sitting at my table watching the preparations. Madame emerges from the doorway and, leaning on her cane, makes her way to where I am sitting. She is carrying a glass of white wine.

"For the appetite," she explains and observes while I take a sip. There is something volcanic hidden in this wine that sends it shooting through the arteries. It is Monday and the Portuguese girls are doing the napkins. Since I have eaten almost nothing for a week except what Madame has brought to my room, my napkin is unsoiled.

"No need," I tell the Portuguese girl. "I have not used it. I'll keep it for another week."

She is distressed. "No, no. Madame Gallant," she says. "You must have a fresh napkin."

"But why?"

"It is the way of Les Acacias. Each Monday, when you receive your new napkin, we know and we rejoice that you will remain with us for another week."

I eat a bit of cheese called Tomme de Savoie. It is strong and hard, with an aftertaste like the smell of freshly cut wood. Another sip of wine and I am through.

▼   ▼   ▼

At midnight I was awakened by the ringing of bells, singing, drums, a fiddle, and one fatal flute. There was the sound of many footsteps on the road. Torchlight moved across the walls. I got out of bed and went to the window to see the procession pass by. Over the lake hung a lone star like the pendant of some ancient Order of Chivalry. All at once—I blame the flute—tears. I could not hold them back. Toward daybreak, there came through the open window the watery song of a bird, then another, and another. Green finches. The jangling of a bicycle bell, the abrasive sound of ashes being strewn on the road. And, out on the lake, someone trying to start a motorboat. There it is again.

▼   ▼   ▼

I haven't told you yet about Monsieur. Every now and then he arrives unexpectedly. I can always tell the moment he has come; the metabolism of the place doubles. And for as long as he stays, a week or two, we are in a state of frenzy. Two steps are taken where before one would do; such a calling out of instructions, such a clatter of crockery and cutlery. I had thought him to be Madame's husband, which assumption was greeted with the rolling up of the principals' eyes and the screams of the Portuguese girls. Even Philippe's chin quivered when he heard about it. So I gather Monsieur is what you might call *un ami de la maison*—a friend of the house.

Monsieur, like Madame, is given to iridescence of wardrobe. The reds! The blues! The yellow-greens! All the rich colors preferred in childhood before maturity dulls the retina. He is tiny, mercurial, with a spruce little moustache and a high silver pompadour. His nose is narrow and curved like a beak and he has something less than hands—fingerlings, I suppose. And the daintiest feet in France. Madame calls him *le perruche*, the parakeet. It is Monsieur's role to ensure that everyone on the premises is talking at once. He can no more live in silence than a cat can live under water. And what roulades of language does he deliver, with such flourishes of lip and eyebrow, and such a repertoire of splendid gestures. When there is no one to talk to, he speaks to the wine. On the terrace he circulates from table to table, swirling a glass, inhaling an aroma and *parlez-vous*-ing a mile a minute. So far as food is concerned, he is worse than I am. I have never seen him eat so much as a single grape. No need. Such a perfect nosegay of a human being lives on his own charm.

▼   ▼   ▼

The light of the lamp hurts my eyes. They are full of hot ashes. I weep for no other reason and so assured Madame, whose expression said she thought otherwise. The next thing you know there was Philippe, bearing an old Roman oil lamp with a pointed lip, into which he had poured wax around a wick. In this bronze, pulsating light, I am perfectly at ease. Just to watch the play of it on my arms makes me feel attended. Such a light is a living presence, like a nurse at bedside.

▼   ▼   ▼

Thirst and fatigue. For the one, since I cannot swallow lately, I go to stand in the slaking sound of the waterfall. For the fatigue, a half hour in the sun restores me. Water and sun—the life of a plant.

▼   ▼   ▼

There is a grand villa with a cherry orchard by the lake, called Les Pensieres. The caretaker, Monsieur le Gribi, a Moroccan, is a friend of Madame. She has arranged for me to go whenever I can to sit on the low stone wall that borders the lake. There is a break in the wall where stone steps lead down into the water. The third step is awash, the fourth submerged. The sound of the water lapping at the stone has the same cooling effect as the wind chimes you hung from the rafters on the back porch. The village itself is empty. I have taken to going there at noon, when the heat is greatest. I share the wall with the lizards and red ladybugs that live among the ferns and wild geraniums that grow between the stones. A pair of crested grebes—like ducks, only with sensible lobed feet and no tails—sit in the water in front of the wall, their long necks straight. Now one, now the other, lifts its rump and dives, only to surface again a minute later at some distance. Then it shakes the water from its head and lies to until something says: Do it again. To fly they must beat their small wings like bundles of sticks, but at courting they are grace itself, sending passionate messages to each other with their beaks and wings and the sinuous twining of their necks.

Can you imagine my happiness when I sit on my wall, satisfying the immemorial desire of hot feet for a cold lake?

▼   ▼   ▼

Philippe has given me something I have wanted all my life, only never knew it—a walking stick. One night a storm swept through the village. What a sight! On the terrace, every tree mad as the Bride of Lammermoor. Over went the tables; the chairs blew about. All at once a loud crack, and down went a large dead branch of one of the acacias. Under my window the next morning, I heard someone say, "Thank God the American woman was not sitting under it. She would have been killed."

"No," said Madame. "*Jamais*. An acacia does not kill."

From the branch Philippe has carved for me a walking stick. That is my idea of a benevolent tree. He stood there gravely watching as I took a few steps with it, to make sure it was the right height, then raised his cap and wished me *bonne promenade*. When I thanked him, he looked down at his shoes. If I could, I'd hang his tiny smile around my neck for an amulet. From Madame, too, a gift—a little leather traveling cup that I can tie to my wrist or belt. Every morning I find it next to my bread and chocolate, filled with an ounce or two of the white wine of Seyssel that is refreshing just to look at. Each evening I return it to the table. When, in the heat of the afternoon, I pour a few drops into my mouth, I feel like one of Bacchus's maidens.

▼　　▼　　▼

For days, a piece of music has been going through my mind. Something I used to play, by Debussy, but not "Claire de Lune." Splendid chords and ambiguities—you would recognize it at once. I heard it yesterday when I tossed a stone into the lake and watched the ripples. When it comes at night I imagine that all of Veyrier is sinking into the lake, the water flowing in and out of every window, door, and chimney and that, come daybreak, it will rise again.

▼　　▼　　▼

This stick of mine has become a guide, and a rather high-handed one, I must say. Each day it decides where we shall walk—one day to the waterfall, another to Les Pensieres, and so forth. Should I try to resist, he turns stubborn and throws his skinny shadow across my path. More often than not, lately, he refuses to come out of the armoire at all, thereby informing me that we shall not be going abroad today. But this morning he said, *Allons-y!* and took me to the little square opposite the church, where once a week the farmers come down from the mountain villages with their produce—circles of cheese, fat leeks, mushrooms, melons of every color, and baskets of little red berries. FROMAGE, said the stick with a kind of wooden insistence, so I approached a woman in a peasant dress who stood with her back to me. When she turned, I had to catch my breath. It was like looking into a mirror that held my image from a year ago: the same hair and yes, the same mouth and chin, even the same mole on the left side of the neck. Only now she is pink and plump and I have purple swatches under my eyes and a dark seam for a mouth. I saw the spark of recognition in her face, too. For a long moment we stared, as though I were gazing into my past and she into her future. Then we both shrugged, laughed, and the spell was broken. When I tried to pay her for the cheese, she refused.

"No, no. It is something that I give to myself."

▼   ▼   ▼

There is another lone woman at the hotel, a blonde with dark eyebrows penciled high on her forehead and a silent-upon-a-peak-in-Darien look on her face that brooks no effort at familiarity. She is always dressed to the nines—silk blouse, high heels—and moves about in a cloud of perfume. Her table is nearest to mine on the terrace. She is accompanied everywhere by a small dog named Bonbon, the size of a toy poodle, only with long, coarse brown hair that goes silver at the tips. Bonbon has a penetrating metallic yip and is dreadfully testy and spoiled. She carries him under her arm to her table and places him on her lap, where he remains throughout the meal. Now and then she offers him a piece of kidney or a bit of chicken from her long red fingernails. *Je déteste le chien.*

The woman occupies the room at the end of the hall on the same floor as mine. Number eleven. What with the roar of the waterfall, I do not hear a sound, not even from Bonbon. This is a perfect house for keeping secrets. I know mine, but what could hers be? She seems to be waiting for something. Or someone. We have not spoken, not even *bonsoir*. Perhaps she senses my antipathy for Bonbon. You know very well my affection for dogs. I have always thought even the most splathery, weather-headed mutt more open to the possibility of redemption than some of our human friends. But here we have Bonbon and I am no longer sure.

▼   ▼   ▼

Louis-Antoine is the village baker. Always he wears that weary look that is the sober badge of office. In Veyrier, bread is a calling. His entire repertoire consists of long, thin crusty loaves made of yeast, water, flour, and salt, the most delicious I have ever tasted. I have been twice now to visit him at his oven, which is an igloo-shaped, igloo-sized brick structure located in the dead center of Veyrier. Every morning Louis-Antoine fills it with well-seasoned oak logs and fills the whole village with the anticipation of fresh bread. His face, beneath the dark blue beret that sits flat on his head, has a permanently scalded look. His hands, too, look boiled, the nails caked with flour. The end of his beard and even his eyebrows are singed. Once a month in the late afternoon, when the oven has cooled, he crawls into the igloo and scrapes the soot. Seen through the oven door, he is a great crouched loaf himself.

▼   ▼   ▼

Last night, when the pain came, I rose from bed and went to the open window. I have never been so close to the moon. It makes you dizzy. There I sat, Hugh, with my back to the moon, combing my hair (the one part of me that is thriving—it has grown very long), combing and combing with long, slow strokes, combing out the pain. I read somewhere that the women of Sparta sat in the moonlight combing their hair until their sorrows went away. It works. I fell asleep while combing, and dreamed a long peaceful dream in which I combed on and on. When I awoke, I was spent, as after a night of passion, and the pain was gone. I can just see that skeptical eyebrow of yours lifting. Never mind. Perhaps the only good thing about pain is that it cannot be shared, and so gives its owner a certain latitude of the imagination. Like my walking stick, this pen of mine goes where it wishes. I have become the servant of my implements.

▼   ▼   ▼

I have become friendly with Nicole, the market woman who looks like me. The other day she took me with her to the small farm halfway up the mountain where she lives with her husband, Auguste, and their baby.

It was a bumpy ride in the old truck, what with the road little more than a gully of stones. Soon enough we were there, but then I was unable to step down from the high seat. It was quite funny the way Nicole came around, scooped me up all matter-of-fact as though I were an ungainly, ill-wrapped parcel (which believe me, I am), and carried me to the porch.

"You are lighter than a baby goat," she said, and deposited me in a chair.

The farmhouse is a little cottage with a steeply slanted roof and a chimney wearing a feather of smoke. There is a barn, an orchard, a field of melons, and a yard with animals. It was exactly as though one of my childhood picture books had come to life.

Auguste is a calm-eyed man who, without turning from his beehives, tossed me two gruff *bonjours* full of promise. *Just you wait!* they seemed to say. Later he gave me a perfect red tomato that precisely fit my palm, and a speckled pheasant's egg borrowed from the nest for my delectation. There is also an old grandmother—in France there usually is—who, having paid her tuition with a lifetime of household chores, now presides over the porch.

The first thing Nicole did was to fetch the baby from its cradle to nurse. Watching the muscular exertion of the baby's pursed lips, his total engagement in the feast, was strangely erotic—like the recurrence of a libidinous dream of my own infancy.

After a while, I felt able to walk into the barnyard. It is a grand thing to be among beasts—cows, goats, geese, chickens. I knew I was welcome when a nanny goat scattered her dry pellets on the beaten earth at my feet. Toward evening, Nicole deposited me at Les Acacias with a small jar of apricot jam she had put up. On my table, it hints at something in a past life that the memory sees but cannot put into words.

▼　　▼　　▼

A night of clatter and rustle, as though a small creature were looking for a way out of my chest. I awoke from an endless dream in which I was wandering through the tunnels beneath a great hospital, wrapped only in a sheet. A trail of my blood stretched behind me. Overhead ran great pipes from which came a filthy gurgling. So narrow and low were the passageways in some parts that I had to crouch and turn sideways. It was hot. I grew more and more faint, weaker and weaker. At last I came upon a door, pushed it open, and found myself in a cool, dark space occupied by stone tables. With my last bit of energy I lay down upon one of them. Imagine my relief to wake up and find myself in my beloved room.

All day I lay listening to the lovely grammatical chant of French rain on the roof. Toward dusk it stopped, and the sky cleared. Slowly the thing on the bed became a body again, tried out its joints to see if they still worked. Enough of them did to let it get itself to the window ledge. In time the moon rose and cast a beam across the lake. I could have walked across it. It is scandalous that such a thing of beauty should have no name in English, nor, according to Madame Durand, in French. To redress the lapse, I have invented a word for *path of moonlight on the water*. It is *lunaqua*. Keep your Hudson River with its heaving current, its gleaming vaporous mornings, its nights of netted stars, and give me the midnight lake at Veyrier with its silver lunaqua. Since I have no other, this world shall be my legacy.

▼   ▼   ▼

Among the things I am shedding is my skin, though with none of the grace of a snake, just shreds and peels of rind. Parts of me are quite raw. Why do they call it shingles? I cannot bear even the weight of the sheet on my chest. Once again Madame has provided: a loose, flowing white cotton gown that covers me wrist to ankle, with a mantle to raise against the sun. Monsieur le Gribi says it is a djellaba. What a strange sight I must offer to the vines and hedges on the path to the lake. I could be an Ishmaelite woman leading out my nomadic, extemporaneous life.

▼   ▼   ▼

Once again, I have visited Louis-Antoine. Bent over his kneading trough, he did not at first see me, and I watched for a few moments his strong fingers pressing, punching, squeezing. Without looking up he reached for the pitcher to add a little more water, then thrust his hands into the pliant dough. At last, I had to break the voluptuous silence with a cough. Louis-Antoine straightened, wiped the clots of dough that webbed his fingers, and drew up a bench for me to sit. One by one, he molded the loaves, laid them out on trays. Like unborn babies they seemed, each with the same unstoppable urge to rise as this belly of mine. When, all at once, the child kicked, and I was reminded that I was not one of Louis-Antoine's loaves, I felt something between disappointment and envy.

▼   ▼   ▼

Where did I read about a plant that flourishes only in places where there is much seasonal rainfall? (Perhaps it was you who told me?) During long dry periods, it extricates its roots from the parched earth, grows dry and weightless until it is lifted and carried by the wind to another wetland, perhaps hundreds of miles away. There it sets down roots and grows green until another drought comes and it must move on. It is the exact description of the life cycle of my mind, which for several weeks now has been aloft on a hot wind with no moist bed in sight.

▼   ▼   ▼

I have been unable to write for several weeks because of the swelling in my hands. How stupid hands are when idle. But now you see that I am once again at my notebook. Here's what happened: Early this morning Nicole came in the truck to bring me to the farm for the day. Auguste was at the bees. One is never out of earshot of their coppery buzz. All afternoon Nicole coaxed the ewes to come and be milked. I must have fallen asleep. When I awoke, there was Auguste, still tending his hives. Nicole went to where her husband was working, reached out, and captured a handful of the bees. She came to where I was sitting. Then, as though it were the most natural thing in the world, she grasped one bee between thumb and forefinger and placed it on my right arm near the elbow. At the sting I jumped, out of pain and surprise. But Nicole smiled and shook her head as though to reassure a child. She took another bee from her fist and applied it to my other arm. Another sting. The rest of the bees, she released and waved away. Within minutes, my arms, which had been cold and lifeless and stiff, grew pink and warm. I felt currents of electricity flowing into my dead fingers, which became, and still are now, limber. Can you see the improvement in my handwriting? When I asked her about it, she gave me one of those tiny smiles in her repertoire and said simply, *"C'est le lait des abeilles."*

▼   ▼   ▼

I have not felt the baby stir for three days. It is strangely still, as though gathering its strength for the ordeal of birth. It is the only thing I dread. Tonight, unable to sleep, I looked at the moon so long that when at last I turned away from it, my eyes in the mirror seemed to glow with the same soft light. Below me the roofs of Veyrier pulsated like the fontanelle of a newborn child. And now I feel suffused with an internal languor, as though I were a cup in which tea leaves were slowly settling, all but one. Soon, soon.

▼   ▼   ▼

I will make this short. What you shall have, Hugh, are one or two of the facts and the truth.

This morning Madame brought me a steaming resinous cup in which herbs floated. "What is that?" I asked, but I knew.

She stood by the bed and watched me sip it to the dregs, then placed an hourglass on the table, turned it over, and left. When the last of the sand had run through, the pains began and Madame returned. She stayed with me the whole time.

All day long, like a deaf woman, I felt, but could not hear, the shrieks tearing through my throat. The child was born dead. When it was over, Madame took it from me.

I didn't have the courage to look, but I named him Louis-Antoine, for the baker and his perfect bread. There are things that, even now, I cannot bring myself to do. I cannot leave behind a nameless child, not even a dead one, in this village where every path, cottage, and beast has a name. I felt no grief, only exhaustion, and the relief at having cheated a voracious fate. All the same, it is hard. Later, Nicole came and combed my hair with great long strokes.

▼   ▼   ▼

A new spot has appeared on my thigh. That makes three. A week ago I used the last of the morphine, but along with it, I seem to have used up the pain as well. Perhaps it has left me for some meatier bones to gnaw. There has been no bleeding for three weeks. I have the feeling that I have passed one trial and am being made ready for another.

▼   ▼   ▼

Monsieur le Gribi has taken me by car to Seyssel, a town on the banks of the Rhône. The river there is broad and wild. No wonder Madame Sévigné was frantic at the thought of her daughter crossing it on a raft. We sat by the river. Monsieur le Gribi drank several glasses of *pastis*. I sipped from my leather bottle.

"You cannot buy such wine in America," Monsieur le Gribi said.

"Why not?"

"Such a wine does not survive a journey. If you try to take it away from Haute-Savoie, it will collapse into vinegar."

"Like me," I said.

We watched the men playing petanque, a game with wooden balls that is midway between billiards and croquet, only played with the hand. The men are of the same tribe—short, squarish, not at all fat, but solid. Topped with berets, their good-looking heads seem to me to have been chipped from the same block of wood by a single-minded clever axe. By the time we returned to the hotel, I had to be carried upstairs. Never mind—such an afternoon was worth the currency.

▼   ▼   ▼

Today I sat on the wall at Les Pensieres in the noonday sun and dangled my shadow in the lake like bait. Leaning over, I gazed until the stony mountain behind the hotel slipped its tether and escaped through the water. That which on earth cannot be, in water becomes.

I must have nodded, because next thing I knew, there was a man before me, with water streaming from his shoulders. He had hard green eyes and a beard of precise curls arrayed in rows like a statue's, and only a pair of black bathing trunks to persuade that he was a mere mortal. I could not have been more startled had a centaur pranced out of the orchard. To me he seemed one of those creatures that are the dream of childhood and for which the adult never stops longing. A sweet-water Triton! It is just as well, Hugh, that you are rid of me. I have become insufferably particular. Now that I have seen a Triton, I would never be satisfied with a mere man.

"You frightened me," I said. "Who are you?"

His name was Luc, he replied, and smiled a smile that went straight through me. *"Je suis plongeur."*

"A diver?"

"Yes."

"What is it like down below?"

"It is cool and green," he said.

He looked at me with something like roguery and tenderness, but without the least ambiguity. I had to lower my gaze to the wall, where, all at once, the tiny ferns between the stones took on a vast importance.

"One day, when you are ready, you can come with me," he said swiftly. Then, *"À bientôt."* I watched him dive into the water, his gleaming body now curvetting above, now submerging, until he was nothing but a lustrous residue churned by the waves. All the way back to the hotel, there was a bright sting in my mouth as though I had just bitten into a crisp young radish.

▼   ▼   ▼

I asked Madame if she knew the diver. A tiny smile flitted.

"I have heard things," she murmured. I asked her to tell me what she had heard, every least detail. Was he married? I wondered. I died to know.

"He does not marry," she replied, and left me.

▼   ▼   ▼

Fever! The way it pulls the skin taut over one's skeleton, like a drum, then beats on it.

Awake and asleep I dream about the lake, endlessly cleansing itself from a thousand springs, from the infusion of melted snow from the mountains, from the rain. It is new each day. What does not change are the hidden forests and chasms, the kingdom in its depths. Looking into the lake doubles the earth, lending it a celestial magnitude.

▼   ▼   ▼

Every few days Nicole comes to Les Acacias, each time bringing me some bit of food. Today, a brown and speckled free-range egg and a cup of stewed apricots. Then I, who can eat virtually nothing, devour what she brings. In her hands, goat cheese and bread turn into Belshazzar's feast. I asked Nicole to tell me exactly where she found the egg. Was it in the marshy field? In the pasture? She had found it in a little patch of blackberries farther up the mountainside, where she had gone to extricate a ram that had gotten caught in the thicket. Madame poached the egg, and minutes later, there I was wiping the last of it from the plate with a crust of bread. And with gusto! When I had eaten, Nicole and Madame together disinterred me from the bed and brought me forth for an airing. Where did they learn this profound courtesy for the flesh?

▼   ▼   ▼

I have now been here long enough to see the lack of religious conviction of the mountain. In the winter he was a Dominican friar with his white cowl. In spring he turned Jewish and wore a skullcap. Now it is autumn, and he has gone Buddhist and shaved his head. In the face of such fickleness, I have clung devoutly to my atheism. There is something to be said for constancy.

▼   ▼   ▼

Quite often the Triton comes from the lake to sit on the lowermost step of the wall. When he does not, I am desolate.

"It is cruel of you to abandon me," I told him. He laughed with delight.

"Throw a little stone into the water. I will know it, even from the farthest end of the lake." So I did just that today. Within minutes, there he was! Rising from the depths, taut, pulsating, his nostrils dilated, blowing off foam. Now that is what I call telegraphy. Twice he has made a cradle of his arms and carried me into the cold caldron of rebirth that is the lake, and each time, I felt the fever leaving my body. How the water hissed and steamed about me! In his arms, water is not another element, only a heavier, darker air. When I am with him, he is absolutely real. When he has left me, I wonder.

▼   ▼   ▼

News! The blond woman with the dog has a visitor. A swarthy man in a fez—a Moroccan, I would guess. This evening he mounted the steps from the road and stood there for a moment mastering the geography and population of the terrace with his marvelously glittering eye, then made his way straight to the woman's table. Such a yipping and growling from Bonbon, whose hackles rose in outrage. It is obvious that man and dog know each other, to their mutual regret. The conversation was unintelligible to me—Arabic? Still I could see by the violent way she worked her eyebrows that she was *blazing*. At one point, the man reached into his pocket and handed something to her, a small packet that he palmed expertly and that she received with equal finesse into her sleeve. And that was that. Smugglers, I say. Or spies. When the fez pushed back his chair and stood to rise, she sank her long red nails into the meat on her plate and offered it to Bonbon. The fez grimaced in disgust and went quickly into the hotel.

▼   ▼   ▼

The man in the fez has come again and gone. All afternoon he and the blond woman stayed in the room at the end of the hall. Once, I imagined voices raised, a muffled commotion. Minutes later, the sound of a car driving away. The noise of the motor had barely faded when it began, a terrible howling from the end of the hall. On and on, without respite, feeding on its impetus, like a fierce wind from the north, subduing even the noise of the waterfall. A naked grief. All night she wailed. At breakfast, the Portuguese girl told me that Bonbon was dead. I didn't like the dog, but, God forgive me, I only wished it away. When the woman appeared, gray and deflated, I would gladly have had it back. It is pitiful to see her sitting alone at her table. Her misery is terrible to behold. Although no one would say, I suspect poison.

But what a rage for the terrific I am developing here! It is what happens in small hotels. The mind goes lurid.

▼   ▼   ▼

If I didn't know better, I'd say that my legs are fifty years older than the rest of me. Still, I cough very little and have even, I think, gained a bit of weight, thanks to the treats brought by Nicole— not the least of which is Auguste's honey, which I have been spooning down. I am on my second jar. Has the beast let me fall for a time from his jaws? If so, I am stupidly grateful. In the morning I emerge, not from sleep so much as from a kind of dazzled rest, and without fatigue.

A Dutch family has arrived. A mother, a father, and four very pale children. I should think fair skin in a child a great nuisance. It shows the dirt more. When I told this to Madame, she split her sides, *"Méchante!"*

▼   ▼   ▼

There is a basement where the Portuguese girls do the laundry. I love to sit at the top of the stairs, where I can inhale the smell of boiling sheets and starch. In the courtyard out back are lines from which the sheets are hung. All at once, Philippe comes across the yard with a great basket of soiled linen. In a second, the girls are at him.

First Portuguese girl: *"Ah, mon cher, mon amant. Venez à moi*—come here you great beautiful ox. I have a kiss for you."

Philippe: *"Taisez-vous."* The slamming of a door, much laughter from the girls.

First Portuguese girl: "Never mind. A bucket of water over the head will cool him off."

Second Portuguese girl: "In a year he will leap out at you from behind the clothesline."

I swear these girls have wine in their veins instead of blood, the hot black wine of Portugal. Later, when they took down the billowing sheets, my own blood stirred at the sight of them draped in linen like souls in ascent.

▼   ▼   ▼

I have fallen in love with the Triton. I know exactly when it happened.

"I am thirsty," I said. Whereupon he ladled clear cold water into his cupped hands and held them out for me to drink. It was precisely then, when my face, like the snout of some small animal, entered that living cup, that I opened my eyes and saw through the pool of water the calluses, like scales, and the markings in the cushions of his palms, it was then that I fell in love with him. I drank like a parched animal.

▼   ▼   ▼

For three days I did not see the blond woman. On the fourth it turned abruptly cold. I looked up from my table to see her standing in the doorway, hesitant, dazed, yet with her eyebrows freshly penciled and her face a mask of cosmetics. Beautifully dressed, as usual. On a sudden impulse, I called out to her.

"Please," I said. "Tonight you must join me." For a moment she hesitated. Then, as if obeying a command, she came and sat.

"I am sorry for your loss," I said. The words unleashed her grief and she began to weep—bawl, really, her chin all snot and saliva. Within minutes, her handkerchief, a tiny square of sheer cotton edged with lace, was soaked. I could not help recoiling.

"He, Bonbon, was the only one I could trust," she sobbed. "The others have all betrayed me."

What could I say? "Yes, yes," I said, and "Ah!" and "I see," the syllables of condolence, which are all one has to offer the inconsolable. What is this *thing*, I wondered, that could turn this woman's face, a face I had thought incapable of expression, into a dripping cistern? What I felt was, I confess, revulsion. But something else too, something akin to envy.

"Come," I said. "We will go to your room." I led her, still sobbing, through the tables. The stares of the other diners, to which she was oblivious, shamed me. In her room, I helped her to undress and put her into bed. In the darkening room, her grief was less visible.

"I am so ashamed," she said.

"It doesn't matter," I told her. "Madame told me that you will be leaving soon. You can leave your shame here with me."

When she smiled, I felt my heart break. How well I know, how completely I understand that we all have things that no one else must be permitted to see.

▼   ▼   ▼

The blond woman has returned to her table, the one nearest mine. Her hand is in a small brown-and-silver muff on her lap. There she sits, gazing sadly down at the lake, absently running her red nails through the fur.

▼   ▼   ▼

This evening the blond woman and I had a talk. I had already left the table and had just passed her seat when I heard her say very quietly, almost a whisper, "Madame."

I turned. She gestured for me to sit. For several moments we sat in silence, inhaling the sweet smell of the acacias. At last she spoke.

"Already it grows cold in the evening," she said. "The snow is piling up on the mountain. Soon it will be winter. I have heard the wolves howling up there."

"There are no wolves," I said. "Perhaps it was the wind." Was she mad? Perhaps, but no madder than I. And more of a woman, who can grieve. (I could not take my eyes from the muff.) Mad or not, she refuses to let go, in the face of all reason, at no matter what cost to her dignity. I am in awe of it. All at once, she reached out and took my hand.

"So cold," she said, studying my palm. I shivered, but not from the cold. "Tomorrow," she said, "I shall go away for good. I want you to have this. I want you to wear it. You must promise to." When I hesitated, she slipped the muff from her hand and placed it around mine.

▼   ▼   ▼

The blond woman left before dawn. At noon, I heard a car pull up out front and two doors slam. A moment later two men, clean-shaven, in fedoras and neckties, climbed to the terrace. They paused, surveyed the empty tables, then strode to the door of the hotel, where Madame appeared, her hands aflutter. I heard the words *gendarmes* and *sûreté* and my heart contracted to a hard rubber ball that bounced against my ribs. I knew at once that they had come for me, that somehow you had traced me, that now, when it was almost . . . I would be snatched up and sent back to you like an escaped criminal. Oh, God, how I cursed you. I saw the two men shoulder past Madame into the front hall. You can imagine my terror. I lay on my bed and heard their heavy foot-steps on the stairs. Then I heard Madame.

"It is a small hotel, mine, messieurs. There is no one such as you describe. Yes, yes, two women alone, but I assure you that neither of them . . . The one has already left. I don't know where."

"And the other?" They were at the door to number eleven. A rattling of keys, a scuffling of shoes, a door opening, a long pause, the door closing. The footsteps came closer. They were just outside my door. Madame's voice took on an edge of granite. She raised it for me to hear.

"Here," she said, "the room of Madame Gallant, an American. I shall open the door for you to see. There will be a young woman lying in bed with her eyes closed. She will not open them. She will not speak to you. I think you will not speak to her, when you have seen." A soft knock. Me, palpitating in the bed.

"Madame!" she called out to me. "I shall open the door for a moment only. N'ayez pas peur—do not be afraid. No one will come in." Oh, my heart! The door opened halfway. I did not turn to see, only lay as Madame had instructed me, with my eyes closed and my hands folded on my chest, like a corpse. In a moment, the door closed and the footsteps receded. Minutes later, I heard the car drive off. Madame's footsteps returned. When she had come into my room, I opened my eyes for the first time.

"It was not for you that they came," she said. "They wanted the other. Number eleven." She smiled faintly. "They are too late."

"But where . . . ?"

"She was not a bad woman. Not at all. She was brave. How she loved her little dog." Madame's glance took in the muff. "Ah," she said softly. "So." Then she helped me to sit up. "Come, we shall go to the kitchen; we shall have a cup of soup."

▼   ▼   ▼

October. And a full moon in every rain barrel. Now, when nothing is compatible with the raw channel my mouth has become, I can still drink a dipper of this water-of-the-moon. It is a year since I arrived in Veyrier. In the mirror, what I see is a head small with disease, the skull imprinted on the skin. The rest is indistinct, clouded as from a coating of mist. A woman's first real awareness of her body, they say, comes through love or childbirth. Maybe so, but for me it came with the discovery of my sickness, when I began the process of separating from it. And what a fragile thing it is, the body. And how absurd to grow so attached to it. I should like to give it up with grace. Not to thrash about like someone drowning, but rather like . . . after the last reverberation of a bell when, in the pure silence, something in the belfry settles itself and folds its wings.

Hugh, I shall not be writing in this journal any longer. I have no more than a dozen words left in me. Too often now my eyes are full of hot ashes; my wrist is like a handful of dice that have been miscast. Just as well. Writing is rather like driving a car; at a certain age, one ought sensibly to forget how to do it. Reading over these pages, I can only wonder why I wrote them at all. They make no sense, tell no story, not the story I had wanted them to. I have called it a journal, but it is a journal only in that it contains no past or future, just a present. And even that is meager. From the many pages I have left blank, I suspect that the real events of this year have taken place behind my back. And so what you will have, since I promised, are a few hieroglyphics scrawled among long empty silences. Make of it what you will.

For weeks I have been awaiting a sign. Just this Monday it was given to me. At breakfast on the terrace I withdrew my napkin from its linen envelope and lo! it was the same one I had used all last week. There were the stains of the wine my trembling fingers had spilled the night before. When I looked up, the face of the Portuguese girl was beautifully neutral. In the doorway stood Madame, one finger pressed against her cheek, a tiny peaceful smile at her mouth. Philippe crossed the terrace carrying a carafe of wine. How he has grown this year, more bone than fat, his broad Savoyard shoulders, his hair ferociously tamed to his scalp, his whole body silent, alert. Yet still upon his face, the sad, comic despair of the teenage male, as though all the distressed maidens of Savoie had been rescued without waiting for him.

I no longer go down to the terrace. For some days now, I have been dizzy. All around me the hotel moves with a lovely fluidity, the way waltzing couples cause the ballroom itself to dip and turn. I am quite pleasantly numb. In my room, I sleep, I sleep, I sleep. Awake, I sleep on. The sun comes through the window and tries to lift my head from the pillow, but I sleep on. Today I dreamed—no, I saw—that Nicole had come to my room. For the first time she has brought no food for me to eat.

"And today?" she asked, her eyes accepting the two small stains of blood on the pillow. Her hay-scented breath was so sweet that she blew out all the hard hours of the night like so many candles.

"Today?" I replied. "Today I want to go down to the lake, to lie on the wall for a while."

I will tell you how she raised me from the bed in her strong arms and helped me to bathe and to put on the clean white loose gown that Madame had laid out. How Philippe came and together they managed me, oiled and arrayed like a bride, toward the lake. How Madame accompanied us to the edge of the terrace, then stood leaning on her cane, gazing after. How Philippe lifted me to the wall, and Nicole set a small pillow under my head. How, at the top of the path, they turned to wave, shielding their eyes from the sun. How above the hotel, the foam of the cataract was bearing a rainbow down the mountain. How I lay in the sun with my eyes closed, no longer able to store up energy like a battery, but now like an animal, listening, waiting. How, after a while, I heard that longed-for splash as the waters parted.

"Is it you?" I asked.

I felt the cool shadow of my Triton. "Open your eyes," he said. When I couldn't, he raised my eyelids with the gentlest touch of his fingers. In his eyes, I could see the dim aquarial landscape, undulant, tossing. His face was as close as the moon from my window. He gathered me up. I heard the sweet palaver of the lake and the stone steps. There was the shock of the water on my skin, my gown filled with it, my hair floating.

"Down," I said. "I want to go down."

"Yes," he said. "You are ready. We will go now. Look! Here are the fish to welcome you, and the birds to see you off." The last sound I heard was the soft applause of their wings. The next moment my head filled with green. A rush, a rapture, a delirium of green.

▼   ▼   ▼

I have asked Madame to send you this notebook one month from tomorrow. She has promised to do so. Tomorrow I will have crossed over. I would not have traded a century for these four seasons in Veyrier, where a single moment is like a year of mortal life and where I have located the wellsprings of a power beyond annihilation.

One thing more, Hugh. Your first impulse will be to come here. Please don't. There will be nothing of me that is reachable here. Madame, Philippe, Nicole—none of them will have anything to tell you that I have not already written. No mournful pilgrimages. Veyrier does not deserve your sighs, your loitering. Let us be.